What Peopl
About *The Stude...*

"Since founding Blackstone LaunchPad, an entrepreneurship network on 46 college campuses and growing, I've had the opportunity to work with and learn from student entrepreneurs for over a decade. This book does a fantastic job of capturing their experiences, painting a full picture of the challenges and rewards of being a student entrepreneur and the important ways in which a school environment can de-risk failure. The pages ahead are full of practical advice for anyone who dreams of running a business, starting a side hustle, or developing life-long entrepreneurial skills. I encourage all students to explore entrepreneurship, and this book is the perfect place to start that journey."

— Amy Stursberg, Executive Director, Blackstone Charitable Foundation

"I wish I had a book like this when I started my company in college. I spent so many hours learning about the process, and I feel this book would have saved me so much time! The stories in *The Student Startup Guide* will inspire you and motivate you to be the best student entrepreneur you can be. Read it!"

— Josh Aviv, Certified Data Scientist and Founder & CEO of SparkCharge

"As Co-Founder and Chairman at Techstars, I've met thousands of student founders over the last fifteen years. But starting a company in college isn't easy, and until now, nobody has truly captured that experience. Sometimes the best way to gain confidence and learn how to do something is to hear from others who've already done it. This book does just that! The stories in *The Student Startup Guide* will motivate and inspire you—you have what it takes!"

— David Cohen, Co-Founder and Chairman at Techstars

"The founding journey can be lonely. This book is invaluable for connecting founders."

— Allen Zhou, UT Austin, Founder of Big & Mini

"A book like this would have created a framework of conviction and hope for me backed by people who have done the job."

— Ben Omarina, Texas A&M University, Founder of Lazarus

"Creating a business when you are a student seems far-fetched to a lot of people. I think the stigma that it is not the right time or that you need more experience to start a business while you are young is the true misconception. *The Student Startup Guide* allows student-entrepreneurs to hear from like-minded people who are currently going through similar issues and help them realize that it is possible. Once you know it's possible, it's game over for the naysayers."

— Abhi Sastri, University of Central Florida, Founder of FLUIX

"There is a serious lack of resources for student-founders. Therefore, the culmination of real stories, guides, and resources included in this book are priceless. This book is something worth investing in not only for yourself, but for your business from the start."

— Katarina Samardzija, CEO and Founder of Locker Lifestyle and PowerToPitch

"When I started Petitas, I had very little entrepreneurial experience. I was really looking for entrepreneurs like me who were in the same boat. Instead, I often found entrepreneurs who were ten steps ahead and couldn't quite remember the wisdom and lessons they gained during their early days. I would have truly valued hearing from early-stage entrepreneurs, gleaning from their experience and learning from their advice!"

— Chelsea LaFerla, Founder, Petitas

"Starting a company was always a black box for me: there were ideas, and there were companies with full staff with nothing in between. I would have loved to have had *The Student Startup Guide* as a resource when I was getting started to know where to look and how the heck you build a company!"

— Marco Loba, CEO of Catena Biosciences

"As many resources as there are out there, they often cater to a wide spectrum of an audience. Students are in a unique position deserving of a unique resource. It's important to hear from founders who were recently in your shoes, and this book supports with exactly that."

— Alyssa Petersel, Founder and CEO of MyWellbeing

"Going through tough experiences is super-hard, especially when you have to figure things out by yourself. This book will be there to guide you through those tough decisions and experiences. A book outlining a plethora of student-entrepreneurs' experiences all in one place will, without a doubt, be valuable to someone out there looking to start something in their college years."

— Anonymous Student Founder

"A book like this portrays the reality of being a student-founder and how we share the same struggles and fears. But seeing how others have managed through university programs is always a great guidance and motivation. Moreover, it helps to make visible the whole process of building a start-up. Creating something from scratch does not always require a big upfront capital investment but rather a creative mindset and a deep commitment to building your solution one step at a time."

— Laura Rocha, Cofounder and CEO of Dathic

"You don't often get the opportunity to have a resource so available to you from people who have gone through the experience of starting a company. Learning from others and hearing what people have done is the single most valuable asset to me in growing my company, and to have so many sources in one book is incredible. I wish I had something like *The Student Startup Guide* when I was starting out."

— Mario Micale, Founder and Principal of Narrative Digital Media

"A book like this would be invaluable to me as a founder. The ability to have an A-to-Z guide on how to start and grow a startup as a student-founder would have been so helpful when I was starting my company."

— Sam Hollander, Syracuse University, Founder of FSCL

"While pursuing entrepreneurship in college, I wished I had peers to discuss the current struggles and situations I was dealing with. A book like this answers the burning questions of a student-entrepreneur, helps fill that void, and would be my go-to resource to help propel my growth even faster."

— Valtteri Salomaki, CEO of EDGE Sound Research Inc.

"There is just so much you do not know. Everyone is around to give you advice, but it's usually not 'in-school specific,' but here it is in one spot!"

— Jason Goodman, CEO of Antithesis Foods

"Founding a startup is incredibly difficult from prototyping and product development challenges to fundraising and team building, all while trying to sort through conflicting advice and opinions. Having a "real-life" guide to startups with actual stories from other founders would help new founders to navigate through complicated challenges and find the right resources and information to learn from."

— Daniel Couser, Founder of Zen Stone

"Having a snapshot of resources from other student-founders while I was pursuing student-entrepreneurship would have been such a solid resource for me! To understand how to balance the time, not feel like you're a complete maniac, and understand the fundamentals to scaling so early on would have been amazing."

— Jamika Martin, Founder of ROSEN Skincare

"This book would have been valuable to us because there is no clear path that defines how to start a company, especially in college. There are so many unknowns that being able to clear even a few of those up would have saved us a tremendous amount of time and stress."

— Jordyn Goldzweig and Sam Brickman, Cofounders of QBuddy

"A guidebook for entrepreneurs who are still in school would have been an incredible resource to me had it existed when I was starting Govern for America. We were lucky to have many great resources at NYU, but getting guidance from this type of book would have likely accelerated our growth and success and helped us avoid those avoidable mistakes that many student-entrepreneurs make in the beginning!"

— Kyleigh Russ, Cofounder and COO of Govern for America

"I wish I'd had this book when I was a student. Even though I wasn't entrepreneur-minded then, realizing it was possible to do something like this would have opened up new doors for me. I hope students will embrace this book and realize they do not have to be limited solely to jumping through academic hurdles or working a 9-5 job but can reinvent themselves now and over and over throughout their lives and careers. *The Student Startup Guide* is a true life startup guide because once innovative thinking starts, it need never be stopped."

— Tyler R. Tichelaar, PhD and Award-Winning Author of *The Nomad Editor: Living the Lifestyle You Want, Doing Work You Love*

THE
STUDENT
STARTUP
GUIDE

Real-World Advice for Launching Your Company in College

Courtney Gras

Foreword by Brad Feld

AVIVA
PUBLISHING
New York

The Student Startup Guide:
Real-World Advice for Launching Your Company in College

Copyright © 2022 by Courtney A. Gras. All rights reserved.

Published by:

Aviva Publishing
Lake Placid, NY
518-523-1320
www.avivapubs.com

Address all inquiries to:
Courtney Gras
www.students-start.com

First Printing, 2022

ISBN: 978-1-63618-085-4

Library of Congress: 2021915150

Editors: Tyler R. Tichelaar and Larry Alexander, Superior Book Productions
Cover Designer and Interior Layout: Meredith Lindsay
Author Photo: Robin Powell

Every attempt has been made to properly source all quotes.

Printed in the United States of America

First Edition

THE STUDENT STARTUP GUIDE

Real-World Advice for Launching Your Company in College

In loving memory of my mother, my inspiration.

She was a rockstar. A self-taught computer programmer, world-traveler, and ultimate organizer-of-everything; she gave up her career for a bigger challenge: raising me (and homeschooling me). She loved working hard and enjoying life even harder. She showed me the spirit of entrepreneurship, and because of her, I am able to write this book today.

I love you, Mom.

ACKNOWLEDGMENTS

This book wouldn't be possible without the wonderful people I've had the opportunity to know throughout my career. The people who pushed me out of my comfort zone but always had my back if I made a wrong turn. The professors, friends, and family who encouraged me to start a company in college, the cofounders who kept me sane, the students who have founded their own companies—what we call student-founders—whom I've met over the years and who continue to inspire me. There are truly too many to list here, but to name a few:

Dr. Tom Hartley, for encouraging me to start my company when I had no idea how.

Rick Stockburger, for handing me a copy of *Startup Communities* by Brad Feld and giving me my first chance to help entrepreneurs succeed.

My Techstars family, for teaching me the power of #givefirst.

All the students who contributed to this book, for sharing your stories to inspire others and generally being *amazing*.

My husband, Devin, for being supportive and understanding while I spent nights, weekends, and evenings at Larry's working on this book.

My mom and dad, for dedicating so much of their lives to building a bright future for me.

Thank you!

CONTENTS

FORWARD

I started my first company when I was a freshman in college in 1983. It failed. I started my second company when I was a sophomore. It failed. I started my third company, Feld Technologies, when I was a senior. We sold it to a public company in 1993, seven years later. Since then, I've gone on to help start a number of other companies, including Techstars, and several venture capital firms, including Foundry Group, where I'm currently a partner.

Over the years, I've learned a lot about what makes an entrepreneur successful. It has nothing to do with age, where you went to school, or what you studied. It has everything to do with your character, what you are obsessed about, and your willingness to focus a lot of energy on creating a new business where one didn't previously exist.

In 1983, when I was working on my first business with three other founders, none of us had any idea what we were doing. We read everything we could find about entrepreneurship, which wasn't that much in 1983. We hunted down other entrepreneurs, and we just tried stuff. We learned a lot, but ultimately, we realized our business wasn't going anywhere.

In my second company, Datavision, we created a fantastic piece of software for performing cephalometric analysis. We partnered with a professor at Louisiana State University (LSU) who had come up with a new technique for this. We automated his process. Never heard of cephalometric analysis? You aren't the only one. We had one customer (the LSU professor), and our deal with him was that he got our software for free in exchange for helping us figure out what to do. We never had a second customer and eventually failed.

In 1987, my cofounder Dave and I almost went out of business three months after starting Feld Technologies. We had some customers, but we had hired a bunch of part-time employees and didn't have any cash. It only took us two months to realize we would go out of business unless we made a profit every month. We fired everyone and didn't hire our first actual employee until two years later. By then, we had enough demand for what we were doing to add new employees over the next few years.

It took me three tries to learn a key lesson, but I eventually realized it. "Create something people will buy from you."

I first met Courtney in 2016, when she was building a startup community in Ohio, shortly after she left the startup she founded as a student. It was apparent that she was eager to help other young founders. I also knew Courtney wanted to make a difference beyond her local community and support founders everywhere—that's when she decided to pursue a position with Techstars. She accepted the launchpad director position in 2018, which she was offered because of her first-hand experience as a student-founder and her evident passion for the work. In this role, Courtney worked with dozens of universities and thousands of student-founders to ensure they had connections to the Techstars network and resources to find success in their entrepreneurial journey. Courtney worked with students from different backgrounds and educational experiences; she listened to their struggles and built solutions to propel them forward.

While doing this work, Courtney collected stories from students working on companies across the globe. Some were very successful, while others decided to move on after college and found fulfilling careers elsewhere, leveraging their entrepreneurial experience.

You, dear reader, get the benefit of Courtney's experience condensed into this book. It is a collection of stories from student-founders from around the world. Here you get the benefit of hindsight from students who started their own companies. Hopefully, many of your questions will be answered, hesitations dissolved, and next steps made clear by reading the following stories.

Since I have worked with thousands of founders, let me share a few tips as you embark on your entrepreneurial journey:

1. Ensure you are working on what you were put on planet Earth to do.
2. Choose your path; don't let it choose you.
3. Learn from everything you do and everyone you meet.
4. Get comfortable making mistakes. Just make sure you learn from each one.

Good luck with your startup!
Brad

Brad Feld has been an early-stage investor and entrepreneur since 1987. Prior to co-founding Foundry Group, he co-founded Mobius Venture Capital and, prior to that, founded Intensity Ventures. Brad is also a co-founder of Techstars.

Brad is a writer and speaker on the topics of venture capital investing and entrepreneurship. He's written a number of books as part of the Startup Revolution series and writes the blog Feld Thoughts.

Brad holds Bachelor of Science and Master of Science degrees in Management Science from the Massachusetts Institute of Technology. Brad is also an art collector and long-distance runner. He has completed twenty-five marathons as part of his mission to finish a marathon in each of the fifty states.

"If one advances confidently in the direction of his dreams,

and endeavors to live the life which he has imagined,

he will meet with a success unexpected in common hours."

— Henry David Thoreau
(and one of my mom's favorite quotes...I had to include it)

INTRODUCTION

Today, more than 60 percent of college students are interested in starting their own companies. If you're reading this book, you might be one of them. About twelve years ago, I was too. I was a sophomore studying electrical engineering, and I didn't have a clue how to start a company. I thought I had to switch majors and study business. Otherwise, how would I be qualified? I was wondering:

- Where do I even start?

- Who on my campus will help me?

- Does my university even care?

- Can they help me?

- How do I build a product?

- How do I raise money?

- Will I have time?

- I have no experience. Will anybody respect me?

- Is now the right time to do this? I have to graduate!

(*The list went on.*)

Maybe you're asking the same questions.

I'm here to tell you you're not alone. You can start a company in college. You don't have to be a business major, your university does want to help you, you can raise money, you can make time, and people will respect you.

If you have any doubts, this book is designed to destroy them. This book is a collection of stories from students who have been there, who have started that company. They've figured out how to manage their time, gain respect, raise money, build products, hire a team, and in general, find a fulfilling career through their entrepreneurial experiences. There's nothing unique about the students featured in this book that makes them any different from you. They came from different places, had different backgrounds, and went to different schools. The only difference between them and you is they took that first step and decided to do it.

By the time you're done reading, you'll have an idea of what it means to be a student-entrepreneur. You'll learn how to stop talking about it and start doing it. You'll learn how to leverage the resources your university has to offer, and how to find other student-entrepreneur resources. You'll learn how to manage your time, not go broke, and maybe even keep your friends. And hey, if things don't work out, you'll learn how to leverage your experience to build the most fulfilling, amazing, super-awesome career ever.

Who am I anyway?

In case nobody has told you this yet, your career probably won't turn out as planned. Mine sure didn't. But I'm happy I was wrong because today I feel like I've had the most amazing career. I've met incredible people, learned more than I could have imagined, and found a job that makes me feel like I'm working for something that matters.

Here's my story:

I never thought I'd call myself an entrepreneur. I went to college for electrical engineering because I wanted to work at NASA, but my sophomore year, everything changed. I was working on a research project with battery technology when a professor encouraged my teammates and me to enter a student pitch competition. We didn't know the first thing about startups, or what a "pitch" even was. But we decided to figure it out.

I worked on the company for eight years—while studying full time and working internships and co-ops, and even after I graduated when I got a job at NASA.

But my story doesn't end there.

MY STARTUP FAILED.

Through failure, I found both my passion and a fulfilling career where I can help other students (and maybe help them avoid the mistakes I made). For the past eight years, I've worked on supporting founders. I worked locally in the startup community in Ohio, then found a home at Techstars—the worldwide network that helps entrepreneurs succeed. At Techstars, I served as Launchpad director and developed programs and systems to support student-entrepreneurs across the globe. I worked with thirty-plus universities and thousands of student-founders from different geographies, backgrounds, and types of universities.

What did I learn?
1. These students are just like you and me.
2. They have stories worth telling.
3. Their stories can help you.

This book is a collection of stories written by the students I've worked with over the years. This isn't just a fluffy motivational book. These stories are real, and they expose the realities of starting a company in college. My hope is these stories will guide you in your entrepreneurial journey, give you an extra advantage, and inspire you to take action.

I wish you all the best in your studies, your career, your startup, and your life!

Courtney

HOW TO READ THIS BOOK

Okay, so you probably know how to read. But I figured you should know how this book is structured so you can get the most out of it:

- Each chapter has an underlying lesson/focus area.

- Each chapter has an introduction to this focus area, with some comments and personal anecdotes from yours truly. (Sorry; you have to hear more from me.)

- The majority of each chapter is a story written by a student-founder from somewhere who built something. Some chapters even have two student-founder authors! Their stories are structured like this:

- Founding story/how they got started.

  - Problem narrative: What struggle did they face in their journey?

  - Solution narrative: How did they overcome this challenge?

  - Top Three(ish) Takeaways: What were their top three takeaways from this experience?

  - #1 Lesson Learned: What is the one thing they learned that really stands out to them?

- Some chapters have a bonus. I've found some amazing experts in the startup-world who will add to the chapter's theme by sharing their top tips and words of wisdom. You'll find these special additions in chapters like the fundraising chapter and the accelerator chapter. These people are seriously awesome—definitely check out their content.

Section One

SHOULD I START A COMPANY IN COLLEGE?

"Don't be intimidated by what you don't know.

That can be your greatest strength and ensure that you do things

differently from everyone else."

— Sara Blakely

You're thinking of starting a company—awesome! But what does that really mean, how do you get started, and is *now* a good time? Ask just about any student who has started their own business in college and they'll tell you starting a company in college is a great idea. But it might not have seemed like that in the beginning. I get it; they had classes to worry about, bills to pay, and parents they didn't want to disappoint.

I went through this exact experience. In my sophomore year of college, I got involved in a project helping an electric vehicle company protect their battery pack. (We were working on stopping it from catching on fire...important stuff, I guess.) We discovered this company wasn't the only company facing battery-safety challenges, and the professor encouraged me to pursue a startup with this soon-to-be-product. All of a sudden, I had to make a choice: Should I fully commit my time and energy to learning all I could about startups, or let it go and focus on my classes? I was passionate about the problem I was trying to solve and already had a great team of other students to work with, so I decided to pursue the company and find all the resources I could to help me figure out what the heck I was doing. I decided the startup was going to be my hobby: I'd spend my free time, nights, and weekends working on it.

That's the key: I decided I cared more about the startup than other activities. I found learning about startups exciting, and I enjoyed meeting other people working on similar crazy ideas. If you feel this is you, the best advice I can give is to make the decision to *commit* to pursuing your idea then take *action* on it.

This section will share stories from students who decided to take the leap. Their stories describe the commitment required to be an entrepreneur in college, how they figured out time-management challenges, and how they overcame their doubts to build something great.

HOW TO START BY TIM AND RILEY

I n this chapter, Tim and Riley describe their experiences starting a company in college and how they overcame challenges by leveraging resources on their campuses and being creative. Tim and Riley had very different life experiences that brought them to entrepreneurship, but they both found ways to make it happen—so can *you*. From their stories, you'll see that your background, family experience, financial situation, and location don't dictate your ability to start something amazing.

FEATURED STORY:
Tim Reazor,
Cofounder, Fifth & Cherry, UT Dallas, MBA and Master of Science in Innovation and Entrepreneurship, graduated 2018 and 2021

Since I was young, I've dreamed of starting my own business. Entrepreneurship runs in my blood—my parents started their own business when I was eight, and I have always had that same spirit.

After college, I had a successful ten-year career as a Marine Corps helicopter pilot, after which I went on to pursue a second career working in a field that had been a long-time passion of mine: stocks and the markets. But even with all of the professional success I achieved, I still felt like I wasn't living up to my full potential. Then, at forty, one year into my second marriage and with my second child on the way, I went back to school.

I have had business ideas my entire life and always dreamed of following through on one of those ideas, but I didn't know where to start. I needed structure to my education, formation of ideas, and networking. I needed a home with an entrepreneurial spirit. I found no better place to realize my dreams than the executive MBA program at The University of Texas at Dallas (UTD) and the Blackstone LaunchPad. This is where Fifth & Cherry was founded.

Going back to school in mid-life is a major undertaking in and of itself. It may take a supportive job/boss willing to give you the time off, and it certainly takes a partner who is just as committed as you are. If you're going back to school with the goal of starting your own business, you need all of the support you can get. I was and still am extremely blessed to have had the resources and support needed to follow my dreams.

Many of my classmates never took their businesses from idea to launch because of age, effort, and perceived lack of support. There are certainly lots of reasons older people can't or won't try to launch a business, and a lot of those reasons are 100 percent valid. But I realized a few things during my experience at UTD and The Blackstone LaunchPad that gave me the confidence to try. As an expert on the non-traditional way of becoming an entrepreneur, I will always remember this: There is no traditional way to become an entrepreneur. I hope the suggestions below help your ideas take flight.

Just like life, this playbook is not perfect, and one size does not fit all. It's certainly not a guarantee of success. This playbook is a guide to help you get started today pursuing your dreams. I'm going to list the top three things you can do right now no matter where you are on your journey. I'm always available to help and answer questions at Tim@fifthandcherry.com.

TOP THREE TAKEAWAYS

1. Get feedback on your idea by surveying. Want to test your idea? The easiest way is to create a non-biased survey and then use Facebook to get answers. Here's how I did this. I wanted to know what the world thought of my handmade cutting boards, which I refinish forever free of charge. I recorded a very bland and fact-based thirty-seven-second video on my iPhone outlining my idea. Then I uploaded the video and ten-question survey to my town's local Facebook group and invited everyone to take the survey. If it's answers you seek, surveying is the most impartial, expeditious way to get them, as long as your questions are actually neutral.

2. Build a community around your idea by writing. I am a huge fan of journaling and documenting the process of starting up a business. You'll see examples of this on both my Twitter profile, @TJReazor, and LinkedIn—search for Timothy Reazor to find me. Writing and journaling as I describe below will have many positive effects, such as building a base of supporters, etc. At first, you'll think no one cares what you're writing, and that may be true. But if you write earnestly and honestly, someone will find value in your work. Then the network effect takes hold and more people find your work. Before you know it, you will have built a community of supporters who are always there for you.

3. Find the nearest campus with a Blackstone Launchpad or other entrepreneurship program. These programs have mentors who want to help entrepreneurs find success, entrepreneurship clubs, and free access to tools, communities, and introductions that could prove pivotal to your startup. My world got exponentially better when I met Bryan, Dresden, Sarah, Steve, and Sarah-Jane; they lead the University of Texas at Dallas Blackstone LaunchPad. They're all mentors to me. When I first stepped on campus, I didn't know how to articulate my business idea or which steps to take to make it a reality. It can be scary to allow yourself to be vulnerable and share your dreams. But these five people welcomed me into their world with open arms and brought me opportunities I would never have had without them.

#1 Lesson Learned: Introduce yourself and your idea to a Blackstone LaunchPad or your local university's entrepreneurial program. The more people who know about your idea and what you're working, the more people there are to help you.

About Tim: Tim Reazor is dedicated to creating the most beautiful and longest-lasting cutting boards on the market from responsibly sourced wood. As a Marine Corps veteran who was deployed three times in support of Operation Iraqi Freedom, Tim understands that the most precious commodity we have is time, and making memories is time well spent.

Tim's story offers one example of how to start a company in college. But each experience is unique. Our next story is from Riley Rojas. Riley didn't just start one company, she started three! Today she has her dream job working at Facebook, but she still enjoys the entrepreneur life by supporting one of the companies she founded. As you'll read, she started with $12 in her bank account. If you think you need to start with lots of money to be a successful entrepreneur, Riley will show you that's absolutely not the case (if you're dedicated).

FEATURED STORY:
Riley Rojas,
Founder, Aptitud,
UCLA, Political Science,
Graduated 2021, Product
Manager at Facebook

I distinctly remember getting my driver's license the day after I turned sixteen. I was so excited to start driving, I thought it was truly the beginning of "living my life." Then I realized what I would actually be using my car for—it wasn't for fun, but to enter the workforce. My dad was absent for the majority of my life, and my mom had enough troubles of her own raising three kids and being a single mom. At age sixteen, when most kids are going to parties and hanging out with friends, I was pretty much an adult providing for myself. I walked to the closest store to my house, TJ Maxx, and applied to be a sales rep. After a couple of months, I realized minimum wage wasn't cutting it. I got a job at a local bank, working from eleven to five while finishing high school in person and online. By the time I applied to college, I was basically a financially independent adult.

I went to UCLA my first year with only $12 in my bank account. As bad as it sounds, I was motivated by money and finances, since I had very little money growing up. My freshman year, I started making and selling tailgate clothes. The brand took off since there was a huge demand for affordable, fashionable tailgate attire. Fast forward three years—from this clothing company, I raised $125,000 in investments, expanded the clothing line to more than fifteen universities nationwide, led a team of more than thirty employees, and built a female empowerment community. The brand is still being run full time by my cofounder and employees.

Now, as great as that last sentence sounds, it came with weekends full of working while all my friends were out partying. It came with a lot of hard conversations, since I had hired my friends, which comes with a lot of challenges. (I remember googling "how to ship a package" when I got my first order.)

Fast-forward to the COVID pandemic. I was going through a lot at the time, like everyone was. As an entrepreneur, I learned that times of great distress bring great opportunities. Again, I looked at where I was and decided to combine what was going on around me with something I was passionate about. I love health and fitness, so with all the gyms closing, I started an at-home fitness brand called Aptitud. In the months since launching the company, I grew the Instagram following to more than 55,000, TikTok to more than 3 million combined views, grew profit margins to more than 80 percent, got accepted into the Techstars Summer Fellowship ($5,000 grant) and Startup UCLA Summer Accelerator ($5,000 grant), and launched on Walmart and Amazon. My biggest takeaway from this experience is: Align your company/brand with what is going on in the "real world."

For example, when thinking about launching a new product, we used the current situation as our guide. Why would a customer want to buy new clothes when they have nowhere to go? They wouldn't, so we pushed back our clothing launch and instead launched an automated text messaging service that motivates people to work out. In the first twelve hours, we had more than 100 people sign up, and in the next couple of months, we will be using this service to push our products. Obviously, this was a much better product to launch in a pandemic since people were staying home and connecting to the world through their phones for a majority of the day.

That is a glimpse into my life over the last three years. As rewarding as it has been, it has been just as challenging. Now, I'm working full time as a product manager at Facebook. It is dream job, and I couldn't have made it here without the experience I gained though my three companies. Now my everyday work is focused on building products for the 3 billion+ users we have. I'm still in the "entrepreneur world" since I am hands-on in the day-to-day operations of the Aptitud, but a majority of my time is spent at Facebook. I'll end with this last piece of advice:

While my clothing company, Izzy & Riley, was still in the early stages, I was also working part-time at a bookstore to make ends meet. During my time at the bookstore, I saw a huge problem. Students rarely sold their textbooks at the end of the quarter. Whenever I see a problem, I think to myself: *If I had a magic wand, ideally what would I do to make this situation easier/better?* That is how I think of 99 percent of my business ideas: as solutions to problems I face. Then I am confident that I know my target demographic (because the target users are people like me). That year, I led a team of four engineers, developed a prototype, and got my own patent. I designed a kiosk machine that allows users to easily resell their textbooks. It is currently being used/tested on UCLA's campus.

It's extremely difficult (obviously) for me to bundle all of my life experiences and hardest moments into one story, but I hope this was a nice peek into what it's like being a twenty-one-year-old female entrepreneur living in Los Angeles. I'm not going to lie—I often feel extremely alone and isolated since I have few people to talk to about the career challenges I face as a young female in the technology industry or the burdens I feel as an entrepreneur with so much student debt. Honestly, what gets me through every day with a smile on my face are my best friends and family who support me. You don't need a lot of friends or family; a couple of solid people will make everything worth it.

I have no idea where I'll end up, but I know I have a genuine passion for creating and building meaningful products that enrich the world. For anyone looking to start a business or become an entrepreneur in whatever shape or form, my best advice is always to surround yourself with people who can support you on those dark/isolated days because that is when you will see the most growth, and as always, it always gets better. Remember, the more losses you take, the closer you are to succeeding. (I remind myself of this every day.)

TOP THREE TAKEAWAYS:

1. There's a *big* difference between being motivated and being disciplined. I am not "motivated" 100 percent of the time. Honestly, I'm motivated probably 20 percent of the time. But the other 80 percent comes from discipline. If you want to be an entrepreneur and run your own show, you have to have the discipline to work for it, to show up every day, and to give it your all because if you don't, who else will?

2. Do your due diligence in checking out the people you are considering going into business with! I cannot emphasize this enough. I have lost some of my closest friends by going into business with them. Be extremely careful whom you choose as your cofounder or close business partner because it will make or break your company (as Steve Jobs says).

3. Don't be scared to create a business in an area where you know absolutely nothing. Do you think I knew anything about creating a kiosk or the textbook resale business? Do you think I knew how to communicate with engineers? I did not. But now I can tell you the textbook resale business is exactly like the stock market, and I can tell you how to build your own app and connect it to actual hardware. The biggest thing you learn as an entrepreneur is that you learn doing.

#1 Lesson Learned: If I could give one piece of advice to another founder, it would be: You can be anything, do anything, have whatever schedule you want. There is no "perfect" entrepreneur. I am not the most conventional entrepreneur—it's all about the process and having confidence in yourself and your idea. My second tidbit: It's always easier when you have people supporting you along the way, especially in those moments of isolation. I wouldn't be where I am or who I am today without the unconditional love of my two brothers, Cayman and Reece, and most importantly my mom. My mom has been my rock and my reason, and she will continue to be my biggest source of inspiration. (Shoutout, Mom!)

About Riley: Riley Rojas is a three-time entrepreneur who is currently working full time as a product manager at Facebook. As a female person of color, she advocates for women in entrepreneurship and women in product management.

DEGREES AND GPAs
BY ABHI AND KATE

One common hesitation I hear from students is: "I'm not a business major. Don't I need to be if I want to start a company?" The short answer is, absolutely not. If you look at the world's most successful entrepreneurs and leaders (think Steve Jobs, Bill Gates, John D. Rockefeller, Richard Branson, Al Gore, Joe Biden, and many more), you'll see that these individuals didn't do well in school at all, didn't have a business degree, or even dropped out. (reference: *Inc.* magazine).

In my journey, I decided to take fewer classes at once so I could still excel while also dedicating time and energy to my startup. I learned I could be an engineer *and* learn business tactics. The key was changing the definition of what I wanted to be: Did I want to be an engineer, or did I want to be an engineer who also happened to be a startup founder? As soon as I shifted my mindset and removed the perception that I could only do one or the other, I was able to excel at both.

In the story that follows, Abhi Sastri shares his experience defining success in entrepreneurship regardless of his grade point average (GPA) and planned graduation date.

FEATURED STORY:
Abhi Sastri,
CEO/Cofounder of
FLUIX, University of
Central Florida (UCF),
Aerospace Engineering,
Graduated 2020

In 2017, at the height of the cryptocurrency mining craze, I witnessed a couple of friends build crypto mining computers. They told me changing from an air-cooled computer to a liquid cooler allowed the system to run cooler and thus increase the hashrate of the miner. (Basically, the hashrate is the speed at which you can mine cryptocurrency.) At the time, I was also an undergraduate research student helping my future co-founder, Eduardo Castillo, with his PhD research. I approached Eduardo with the idea of creating a better liquid cooling solution that cryptocurrency miners could use to increase revenue. With his knowledge in heat transfer and fluid dynamics, we set out to develop such a technology and applied for the UCF I-Corps Program. After months of researching the customer base (going through a customer discovery process of interviewing Crypto Miners, Gamers, Server Farms, and finding out their pain points) and working to develop a prototype, we found our customer group was too volatile, changing rapidly based on the fluctuating value of virtual currencies. We decided to pivot after the cryptocurrency market crashed because many of the miners we spoke to were also PC gamers looking for better performance and aesthetically-pleasing liquid cooling systems. These PC enthusiasts enjoy presenting their custom-built PCs. We introduced a wall-mounted frame they can use to build custom PCs and show off their creation like a piece of art. High-octane gaming required them to keep their custom components cooled during the heat of battle. After graduating in 2020, and initial sales in the retail markets, we were approached by a High-Performance Computer Manufacturer, who asked if we could incorporate our patent-pending technology into an all-in-one solution for their business. Now, FLUIX has branched off into solving the problem of inefficient cooling and increased footprint of data centers. As of October 2021, we are testing with server computer manufacturers and raising seed capital to fund inventory.

Entrepreneurship is tough to navigate while in college due to pressure from parents about doing well academically and the competitiveness of finding and preparing for a career. For me, growing up in an immigrant Asian family, education was the primary focus, instilled in me from a young age as the path to success. I believe many people go to college because they do not really know what they want to do (which is normal) or because they are being pressured by family. In my case, I just thought it was the path forward. Luckily, I had parents who let me choose my major. I chose engineering because it let me work with my hands on technical solutions and use my creativity to build and make things (things I loved doing since my first Lego set, helping my brother fix cars, or taking apart computers). To be successful in school takes a certain dedication and time commitment. I realized that in the first few years of university, I lacked this dedication and commitment to do well because I found more interesting activities than my classes. As my GPA plummeted, and I lost some scholarships, I realized I had dug a figurative hole for myself. I had pushed back my graduation by at least two years. More on that later, but I realize now that entrepreneurship is different from school. It does take dedication and commitment, but the workflow is not dictated by a structured metric like grades or a minimum GPA. Entrepreneurship is dictated by other factors such as your ability to solve problems, provide solutions, sell your product/service, or make people aware of how and why your business is helping the world.

Building a business does not require academic success or a certain GPA because, at the end of the day, you, your customers, and the market you serve dictate how successful you can be. The best thing about entrepreneurship is there are many problems in the world, and each comes with a variety of customers you can find solutions for. The possibilities are truly endless.

In the beginning of my sophomore year, while playing basketball in the gym, I met an entrepreneur who had recently launched a product in the beverage industry. He made a proprietary wellness & zen beverage, and he was the first to use kava extract to revitalize the mind and alleviate fatigue after strenuous activities such as working out or after a long day of work and study. This entrepreneur was also a ten-year Army veteran who was excelling in school while working on his business. From hearing his stories, I had developed a passion for solving problems through a product, and I was determined to create something. I wanted to create a venture that leveraged my affinity for creating things and solving technical problems, so I decided to apply myself in school and develop my technical skills in engineering and soft skills such as networking, professional development, and sales. I introduced myself to like-minded individuals who also wanted to build something, and I found the determination to do well in school because I realized my purpose. I wanted to build a business to share this opportunity with others. I found determination through purpose—not through academic success, GPA, or a degree, but through how well I can solve a real-world problem. The pressures of school are taken out of the equation as the structure of curriculum and grades is replaced by a more creative and spontaneous strategy in entrepreneurship. School might be measured by grades, but business is predicated on how well you solve a problem, how much value you bring to others, and how you bounce back after a failure.

TOP THREE TAKEAWAYS:

1. Don't measure your success by your school's ruler. Create your own metrics and stick to them. Your success is dictated by you—that is the truth.

2. It might be tough finding your path in the beginning—that's okay. Unlike school, which follows a set schedule and timeline, entrepreneurship is the long haul, meaning you have to be fast in your daily activities, but take time to think long term because it will take a while before you ever see a return.

3. If you know school is not for you, then don't waste your time with something that you will regret. Double down on what you want to do, but remember you will need not just the determination, but resources, access to information, and skills to succeed. It is easiest to do this while you are young.

#1 Lesson Learned: Find your own metric of success, stick to it, and know that you define your own path.

About Abhi: Abhi Sastri is a UCF aerospace engineering alum, now CEO and cofounder of FLUIX, LLC. FLUIX is a company dedicated to developing workstation liquid cooling solutions to reduce data processing time and save money for Architecture, Engineering, and Construction clients. Abhi is an avid PC gamer, content consumer, and amateur content creator.

Now let's hear from Kate Madden as she shares her journey starting a company with her sister. She describes her perspective on maintaining good grades and overall performance in school while managing her startup.

FEATURED STORY:
Kate Madden,
Cofounder and
Head of Global
Sales, FenuHealth,
University College
Cork, Food Marketing
and Entrepreneurship,
Graduating May 2022

At the ages of thirteen and fourteen, my younger sister Annie and I decided to enter a national science competition known as the BT Young Scientist and Technology Exhibition. This exhibition occurs in Dublin, Ireland, every year and allows secondary school (high school) students to showcase their scientific ideas to the nation of Ireland and abroad. Our project was all about finding what flavors horses pre-ferred, which would encourage them to eat their food if they stopped doing so if they were sick. We showcased the results of our project at the exhibition in 2015, where we ended up grabbing one of the top awards! This catapulted us into both national and international media, which allowed our idea's popularity to grow. About two months after the exhibition, we decided we would convert our science ideas into a business. This business became "FenuHealth." Our first big adventure was travelling to Essen, Germany, to the largest equine trade fair in the world, called Equitana. Here, we were introduced to global distributors and potential customers, even though we only had a product prototype at the time. The interest our products received encouraged us to move quickly and get our first product on the market: FenuFeast, which encouraged horses to eat their feed. Shortly after, in 2016, our largest product development began: FenuSave that helps with stomach problems in horses. This product exploded on the market and is still our most popular product to date.

Being a student and entrepreneur has its challenges. Many of these challenges arise from simply not having enough time in the day. Getting an education while also growing my international business, I was often asked why I didn't just focus on one. I never understood why people were trying to convince me to choose one because, once you are organized, you can do anything. Being a student-entrepreneur, you have a different style of thinking from your peers, which many simply do not understand. The simplest way I can explain it is that many student-athletes make time to play their sport and maintain good grades. Well, I do the exact same thing, except my sport is my business. Once I simplified it, people began to understand. Before when we were told it was silly or foolish not to give 110 percent to our education, we accepted people's opinions, whereas now, we can turn around and say we give 110 percent to our education and our business, and that is why we are so successful. Being in the business world means you are working alongside businesspeople who only have one job, and once it is done, they can go home. For us, we basically have two full-time roles, which can be difficult for others to understand.

Most problems, including running a business while in school, are simple problems that call for a simple solution. Our simple solution is time management. The beauty of efficient and effective time management is that it gives you opportunities to achieve and maintain everything you want. One day when I was traveling from college to a business event, I heard something on the radio that helped me understand the importance of time management. It said: "People are not designed to multi-task. The word multitasking comes from the creation of computers. Computers can hold the internet, send an email, and create a text document all at the same time—that is multitasking. People are designed to do one task at a time—that is called single-tasking." As I listened to that piece of advice, it all became very clear to me that once you manage your time efficiently, you can complete any task to the highest standard once you give it 110 percent of your time and effort while trying to achieve it. Time management is a phrase we all hear and "learn" about in school, but when we have to put words into action is when we truly understand the meaning and importance behind it.

TOP THREE TAKEAWAYS:

1. The advice I would give is do what you want and do not always listen to what other people tell you is the right thing to do. If it is possible for students to maintain good grades and play sports, then it is just as possible for students to maintain good grades and grow an idea into an international business.

2. Secondly, work on time management. Being able to say when you will and will not have enough time for a certain task will allow you to get other tasks completed. I believe there is nothing worse than beginning a task and not having enough time to complete it to its fullest potential. Take your time.

3. Finally, never forget that "multitasking" describes computers. It was the unique selling point for computers, not humans. Set up your time to complete single tasks rather than putting yourself under pressure to do more than one task at a time and ending up performing them all poorly.

#1 Lesson Learned: Anyone can be a CEO, but not everyone can be an entrepreneur.

About Kate: Kate is a third-year student at University College Cork, Ireland. At fourteen, she co-founded a business called "FenuHealth" with her younger sister Annie. FenuHealth supplies a range of products to the equine industry, particularly products for stomach problems in horses. They now have nine people on their team and sell to fifteen countries.

TAKE ACTION BY VAL

As a student, you probably find yourself wondering how to get started in entrepreneurship. Maybe you have ideas written in a notebook, but you are just afraid to act on them.

What if you fail? What will your friends and family think? How will you learn how to run a business?

What I learned through my personal journey is that you just have to do it. Start working on your idea and convert ideas into action. It sounds simple, but in the act of acting, you'll start to learn without even realizing it. The big tasks ahead will start to feel more doable than before you started, and you'll start to gain confidence.

The idea of working on your company might feel daunting, but the following story from Val will help motivate you. Val decided to act on ideas, but also to take the time to reflect on failures and pivot when needed.

FEATURED STORY:
Valtteri Salomaki,
CEO, EDGE Sound
Research, Inc, University of
California Riverside, MBA
in Information Systems and
Marketing,
Graduated March 20, 2020

When I was in high school, all I dreamed of was starting my own business. I used to watch *Shark Tank* religiously because I was always fascinated by all the amazing inventions presented on the show. This encouraged me to start writing down a bunch of business ideas in a notepad; however, I never pursued the ideas because I was intimidated by the idea of starting a business with zero experience and afraid of judgment from my peers if I failed.

Then, unfortunately, my family was hit hard financially, and my world turned upside down. I felt hopeless not being able to provide for my family and told myself I would never allow a similar situation to happen again. In that moment, I decided I would start taking matters into my own hands and not let any personal excuses hold me back from pursuing my aspirations.

Instead of just talking about ideas or writing them in a notepad, I finally decided to act on a tea import/export business my brother and I had been discussing for a while. We mapped out a timeline, prepared a budget, and created a marketing plan, and we were off to the races. While this venture eventually failed, it did still make us a profit, which encouraged me to pursue other ideas I had written down in that notepad years ago.

What did I do next? I took some time to reflect on why my idea had failed. I was motivated to improve myself by identifying any knowledge gaps and building multiple side hustles to gain the necessary experience and skills to give any subsequent business idea a better chance of success.

Over the next three years, I worked nonstop to test, learn, and improve business ideas in my spare time. I did everything from designing tattoos, creating a clothing brand, building a gaming YouTube channel, and conducting market research for other businesses. Many of these side hustles failed; however, each failure pushed me to learn faster and gain expertise in areas I would never have learned about at a university.

Fast-forward to February of 2018. I was just about to complete my bachelor's degree in business administration at the University of California, Riverside, and was preparing to start working toward my MBA. I was completing market research for a project, and I stumbled upon a big opportunity in my local market.

Technology applications had helped grow mid-sized to large enterprises; however, small businesses lagged behind due to the difficulties of adopting technology and understanding how to succeed in the digital world. Having learned the ins and outs of digital marketing and technology integration from my previous ventures, I knew exactly how I could help bridge the technology gap for local small businesses. This led to the development of Free Logic, Inc., a digital strategy consultancy based in Riverside, California.

Soon after, I began working on a few music projects with a doctoral student at the University of California, Riverside, named Ethan Castro. We grew a strong relationship, and he asked me to help with his dissertation project, which focused on new audio technology. I was surprised when, in under two months, I was onstage presenting at the CES Techstars University Pitch Competition in Las Vegas, Nevada, and six months later, I left my tech job to work full-time on building a hard tech startup called EDGE Sound Research, Inc.

In under two years, both these ventures came to life; however, they were really six years in the making. If I had not taken the initial leap and built a company with zero experience, I would not be here today telling my story.

TOP THREE TAKEAWAYS:

1. It is never too early or too late to start working on a venture. The most important thing is to act on an idea and see where it leads.

2. Be comfortable with the concept of failure and always focus on learning from your experiences. Most startups fail, but that does not define the entrepreneur. How you react to failure is what matters most and will determine if you succeed in the end.

3. Do not get caught up with what your peers think about your idea. It is your idea and only you need to believe in it. Never let friends, family, or anyone else discourage you from trying.

#1 Lesson Learned: I will end this chapter by offering any student-founder struggling to act on their first venture idea one final piece of advice. Entrepreneurship is not a profession; it is a lifestyle and a journey you must embrace. It will be difficult at times. You will feel lonely, and you will have to make hard decisions. But to get started on this journey, all it takes is the courage to do one single action to move an idea forward, such as join a pitch competition, write a business plan, buy a domain name, etc. You will be amazed by all the new opportunities that will arise and all the support you will get from entrepreneurial networks. And you will feel great personal gratification when you no longer just talk about your ideas but see them become a reality.

About Val: Valtteri (Val) Salomaki is an MBA graduate from UCR in information systems and marketing. He is the cofounder of EDGE Sound Research, Inc, a new audio tech company that helps users to both *hear* and *feel* sound in high definition, and Free Logic, Inc., a digital strategy consultancy helping small businesses, startups, and nonprofits. Val co-founded both ventures as a student. He aspires to grow the entrepreneurial ecosystem in the Inland Empire (Southern California), and support other entrepreneurs on their journeys.

THE STUDENT ADVANTAGE BY CANDACE

We'll close out this section by coming full circle back to where we started with the question: "Is it really a good idea to start a company while you are in college?" Hopefully, by now you've read a few stories that convinced you it's possible. Here are just a few ways being a student helped me and my startup:

1. **Student pitch competitions:** There are *tons* of pitch competitions for students. (I've listed as many as I can in the resource list for this book.) I've known students who completely funded their companies just from student pitch competitions.

2. **Access to other students:** Other students could be cofounders, first employees, or even interns. This is a great way to get free (or close to free) help. You're surrounded by talent on a university campus!

3. **Access to expensive stuff:** You'll likely have access to lab space, expensive test equipment, prototyping supplies, etc. This can save you lots of money and time.

4. **Access to free/cheap legal help:** Many universities have a "legal clinic" where law students can practice their craft; by using the clinic, you get the benefit of not paying for services like operating agreements, articles of incorporation, and much more.

5. **Support with patents:** As I discuss in more detail later, your university can handle the patent process for you (and pay for it).

6. **Access to an entrepreneurship center:** Most universities now have entrepreneurship centers that offer bootcamps, accelerator programs, mentoring, pitch competitions, and more. As you continue reading, you'll notice that many of the student-founders featured in this book took advantage of their university's entrepreneurship center.

7. **Access to education:** Whether you want to brush up on your accounting skills or take a marketing class, as a student, you're in a perfect position to learn as you grow your company.

If you aren't a believer yet, I bet Candace will change your mind. Candace offers great tips for leveraging your student status to help with your startup. She unpacks how you can work with other students, professors, and alumni to move your company forward.

FEATURED STORY:
Candace Walker,
Founder and CEO,
Generation Connect, Inc.,
USC Iovine and Young
Academy, MS: Integrated
Design, Business and
Technology,
Graduated 2020

I am the founder and CEO of Generation Connect, Inc., a social impact company bringing together teens with seniors for engagement, enhancement, and entertainment services. Our founding team consists of three women of color who met during graduate school. Together, we are a passionate and well-functioning team capable of leading our startup to success.

At the bright young age of fifty-something, I decided to return to school to earn my long-awaited master's degree from a highly accredited university. Although I had attended a locally acclaimed accelerator program, I felt having a degree would better position me and the business for eventual success.

I was coming off a failed attempt to launch a startup, and I knew I didn't know what I needed to know to make the enterprise a success. Somewhere along the way, the knowledge I had accumulated from decades of media management and television production didn't matter in this new era of fast tech and unicorns (privately held startup companies valued at more than one billion dollars). Since nothing beats a failure but a try, I needed the type of knowledge that would convince investors I was worth the risk. So, in the words of celebrity life coach, Iyanla Vanzant, "I needed to pull up my big girl panties and get to work."

I think the key word in this chapter is *leverage*, the ability to use (something) to maximum advantage. The definition takes on new meaning when adding the word student behind it. How can a person with a seemingly powerless position have any advantage? Students are typically viewed as empty wells who have enrolled in an institution of higher learning to become filled with knowledge and fulfilled. A common belief is that only after completing a rigorous academic curriculum can one present themselves as knowledgeable enough to have any form of leverage. But in the fast-paced world of startups, if students wait until after graduation to take advantage of their newfound skills, they will probably have missed an opportunity to get a jump on the game.

As a resident of Los Angeles, I soon turned to the University of Southern California for several reasons. It had enough prestige without being stuffy and enough clout to be cool. I applied and was accepted into the Iovine and Young Academy's (IYA) Master of Science in Integrated Design, Business and Technology program. Slightly nervous and a little scared, I threw caution to the wind and was hellbent on making the most of my student status by not just taking classes and getting the degree, but by capitalizing on the school's name and notoriety. After all, the University of Southern California and all its Trojan pride boasts about its alumni network as one of the top features of the school. Sure, it would be nice to meet the iconic founders Jimmy Iovine and Dr. Dre, but if not, borrowing their name to knock on doors would have to do.

Once I was in a school program, it was time to get a better understanding of the culture, my classmates, professors, alumni, and other resources offered by the esteemed institution where I would be spending the next couple of years. The people and programs around me would be the real indicators of how well I could leverage the school's name and all of its accolades.

Classmates

It was important for me to immerse myself in an environment with like-minded individuals determined to get the most out of their time and money. I also knew my classmates were accomplished in their individual fields, from technology to investment banking and design. Working collaboratively with them meant I would be able to expand my knowledge and my contacts. Students came from all over the nation and many other countries. They, like me, would learn how to effectively work together, build a team, and foster meaningful connections.

Professors

The student-professor relationship is one of the most important connections to establish while at any college or university. Professors not only assign grades, but they often have specialized skills and real-world knowledge about the subject matter they teach. The faculty at IYA, as with other institutions of higher learning, typically have extensive resumes with experience at key corporations and other organizations. By fostering a solid rapport with instructors and garnering their support, students can often gain advisors and other key contributors to their enterprises free of cost and without giving up equity. I was fortunate enough to receive essential introductions to important people in my professors' networks. These introductions resulted in immeasurably valuable advice and tutelage beyond the classroom. Because my professors gained an understanding of my company's mission, they provided valuable assistance in strategizing a plan that would maximize my team's efforts.

Alumni

According to USC records, more than 437,000 living alumni are in the Trojan Family with positions of leadership all over the world. A strong and active alumni organization can lead to unforeseen opportunities for you and your startup. By reaching out to your school's alumni association, you can expand your network tenfold with just a few clicks. One of the best tools for quickly sorting and prioritizing possible matches for your specific need is LinkedIn. Simply search your school and other keywords to find a list of relevant alumni you can approach for overall help, additional information on a specific topic, and possibly an introduction to someone in their network. However, before asking for a favor, try to establish a rapport. Do your research. One of the best ways to meet an alum on LinkedIn is to ask them a specific question about themselves or their personal experience. Most people will not refuse to help someone if they can do it quickly and easily. Still, sometimes you have to be persistent and follow up more than once to get a response. But it's worth the effort and brings you closer to connecting than reaching out to someone with whom you have nothing in common.

Once I understood these resources and their value, it was time to see how effectively I could leverage them. Below are two examples of scenarios in which I used my student status and school prestige to gain an advantage:

1. **Business Development**
   a. After pivoting away from my original startup idea and working on Generation Connect instead, I contacted alumni and other professionals serving either teens or seniors to gather data and gain important insights I otherwise would not have had access to. By using my student status to justify research requests, I was able to schedule informational interviews and gain access to market data I still use today. This information helped inform my early decisions on defining our target market and go-to-market strategies, and it allowed us to make connections and establish relationships with individuals who have now become advisors.

2. **Making myself a relevant founder in today's startup ecosystem**
   a. Now that I have graduated, I have continued leveraging my school's reputation and influence. Our team has received votes of confidence based on our school affiliation and its intensive program on several occasions when applying

for accelerators or other funding. Since most accelerator programs (three- to six-month intensive programs for launching startups) value team above other aspects of early-stage startups, having worked collaboratively in a grad school program helped. And although we are not like past startup teams, we are prepared to defy the odds as we work to build an awesome company.

TOP TAKEAWAYS (Candace has a lot.)

1. Have a plan!

2. Research the power players, both within the institution (professors, deans, and other faculty) and externally (recent grads and older alumni), who are making moves.

3. Use LinkedIn as a tool to connect with those you want to emulate or get advice from. But remember to establish a rapport before asking for a favor.

4. If possible, get the school's newspaper, newsletter, or other publications to write about your startup. It will serve you well later when trying to sell your story to larger news outlets.

5. Share your personal why story with as many teachers, deans, and administrators as possible. Get their buy-in and support. It's even better if they become your champion. Third-party recommendations are way more powerful than touting your own achievements.

6. Set aside time to make connections. Launching and running a startup is demanding. Doing it while in school can be overwhelming, so using your spare time effectively is essential.

7. Use your startup for as many class assignments as possible. Whether creating business plans for your finance class or designing wireframes (a visual guide that represents the skeletal framework of a website or application) for your computer science class, work on your enterprise at every turn.

#1 Lesson Learned: Today, leveraging my student status has evolved. I no longer approach people and situations from a position of naiveté and inexperience. Instead, I forge ahead with humility and gratitude, leaning on my credentials with confidence that my team and I have completed the academic require-ments not just to graduate and become part of the alumni body, but also to fulfill our life's purpose.

About Candace: As a mother of a millennial and two GenZers, and the primary caregiver to her mom, Candace Walker is a champion of multi-generational experiences. She currently serves as the CEO of Generation Connect, a startup bringing together teens with seniors for mutual social, economic, and emotional benefit. The company was founded while Candace was pursuing a Master of Science degree from USC's Iovine and Young Academy. She gradu-ated from there in 2020 with two of her company's co-founders, Jamae Lucas and Julianna Avalos.

Section Two

HOW DO I START A COMPANY IN COLLEGE?

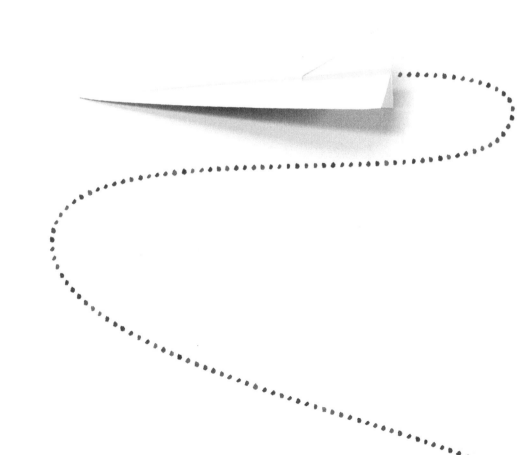

"You don't learn to walk by following rules.

You learn by doing and by falling over."

— Sir Richard Branson

Deciding you want to do something is the easy part. Actually doing it is another story. When I started a company in college, it didn't happen overnight. It took months of research and talking to people who could introduce me to other people who could maybe find the right person to talk to about, say, finding a mentor. I remember thinking to myself, *Is this it? Am I really an entrepreneur now? Because it feels like I'm doing a whole lot of nothing.* But I was wrong. I was doing something—it just wasn't the cool, flashy parts of entrepreneurship we see on television. I was researching, learning, and assembling all the ingredients I needed to start my company. If you're reading this book, you might be at the same stage. Congrats! You are an entrepreneur—you're working on your company right now by reading this book.

If you're like me, you're also a little overwhelmed right now. There are so many questions:

- How do you find the right cofounder?

- How do you raise money when you're a student; will anyone respect you?

- How will you make time?

- How do you find a good mentor?

- How do you know if you should patent your product?

And the list goes on. You could do what I did (learn as you go, talk to tons of people, read a lot), and that's fine. But I hope this section will answer some of those questions and save you some time. Through their stories, the student-founders featured in this section will tell you how they did it. How they built a prototype, how they got their first round of funding, etc. We also have some special guest contributors in this section—experienced entrepreneurs who will add their top tips, and hopefully, save you even *more* time.

Let's start a thing!

GET CREDIT BY JORDYN AND SAM

To kick off this section full of practical tips for starting a company in college, we have a great story from two startup founders that covers all the bases. We'll dig into many of the topics they reference in the chapters that follow, such as how to manage your time, how to find funding, and how to leverage your student status when starting your company. One tip Jordyn and Sam offer is about how they were able to gain college credit for working on their startup. I was able to find ways to earn credit for my company, too, even if it was indirectly. I decided to take entrepreneurship classes at my university and used my startup as a case study for the class. In a way, I got credit for working on my startup.

This is just one of the many hacks you'll learn about in the coming chapters. Enjoy.

FEATURED STORY:
Jordyn Goldzweig and Sam Brickman,
Cofounders, QBuddy, Cornell, Computer Science,
Graduated Fall 2020

Starting as juniors at Cornell University, we worked for more than a year on a startup aimed at helping students meet people in class they could collaborate with on schoolwork. When we were sent home from school in March of 2020 because of the pandemic, we noticed how lonely and isolated people felt and realized that what we had originally built to connect students could be used to connect people of all ages who were stuck in their homes due to social distancing guidelines. We had the idea to start a new website called "Quarantine Buddy" and pulled two all-nighters to launch an incredibly basic website consisting of just a form for users to enter their info and a brief description of themselves. Since we had no money to market the platform and knew the pandemic was the big news story of the time, we realized we could leverage media coverage as a free way to get initial users. We contacted every news station we could to try to get them to cover the story. Within a month, we had been featured on *Live with Kelly* and Ryan, *CBS This Morning*, and *Time Magazine*, helping us accumulate 10,000-

plus users. This all happened before we even had the product fully ready and before spending money on marketing, and from there we were able to rebuild our product through successive iterations as we grew our user base.

As full-time computer science students trying to launch a business, we lacked two critical resources: money and time. When we first started, we had no funding. On top of that, we were each taking seventeen-and-a-half credits with extremely intensive workloads each quarter. We were both involved in a variety of clubs and other extracurricular activities, leaving little time to work on the company.

To find time to work on our startup full time while also students, we designed our course schedule strategically—aligning our credits to ensure our studies allowed us to do relevant work on our startup. These classes ranged from independent research credits, designing technology courses to entrepreneurship classes. Each class counted toward our degree requirements yet was project-based, which allowed us to use the opportunity to work for our startup while receiving credit. Additionally, we were able to get research credit through Cornell's computer science department, which ensured the students on the team got course credit for working with us. This allowed us to build our team without having any money to hire talent.

Without money, we found ways to use the free resources available on campus and find non-dilutive funding methods uniquely available to students. (Non-dilutive funding is any capital a business owner receives that doesn't require them to give up equity or ownership.) We ultimately accumulated more than $50,000 of initial funding by applying for as many pitch competitions, fellowships, grants, and student accelerators as we possibly could.

We were also able to launch and test our ideas quickly and cheaply through scrappy minimum viable products (MVPs). Having minimal time and funding, this was critical for us. When we first started QBuddy, a website aimed at matching people together for friendships, we wanted to get it up and running as quickly as we could, so we made a website using Wix and launched two days later. When we launched, we didn't even have a matching algorithm to form the pairs of buddies. Rather than waiting for the algorithm to be completed, we manually matched people using spreadsheets, working every Saturday for the first two months we were operating QBuddy. We would sit for hours sifting through thousands of people and forming the optimal pairs by hand instead of waiting months for the algorithm and website to be completed. This allowed us to accumulate our initial user base and test and iterate our idea months before we otherwise would have if we had waited for the algorithm.

Finally, we learned early on that playing the student card really helps. After sending cold email after cold email only to be rejected, we began to leverage our student status. It's shocking how adding the words "Cornell student" in the subject of an email instantly drives up the response rate. On top of that, playing the student card opens up the door to free resources. Because we were students, we found time after time that people and companies were willing to provide us with software, cloud services credits, and other resources for free, which otherwise would have been extremely expensive.

TOP FOUR TAKEAWAYS

1. Play the student card. You'd be surprised how much being a student helps in getting people to respond to your email and talk to you.

2. Ask for things—the worst thing that can happen is they say no. Just by asking we were able to access many resources for free.

3. Take advantage of student funding opportunities (i.e., pitch competitions, student fellowships, etc.). A critical component of doing this successfully is taking the time to practice telling your story. What we've noticed about these competitions is that it's not necessarily the best business that wins, but rather the business that is best at telling their story and selling themselves as a team.

4. Find ways to launch as fast and cheaply as possible. This is common advice, but it is especially helpful for students who lack time and money. Rather than building a full product before launching, find ways to test your idea through scrappy MVPs.

#1 Lesson Learned: With limited time and resources, being scrappy and resourceful and making the most of what you have is critical to succeeding as a student-entrepreneur.

About Jordyn and Sam: Jordyn and Sam were both Cornell computer science majors who graduated in the fall of 2020. They have worked on a variety of startups in the past while in college, one of which was an education technology platform that is now used at fourteen universities and another which they sold.

CUSTOMERS
BY ALLEN AND (ANOTHER) SAM

As a student, you may wonder how to get off campus and connect with potential customers. Finding customers, aptly called customer discovery, is one of the most important first steps in forming your company. Through this process, you learn if your business is viable. To read more about the process and why it's important, check out the Techstars Entrepreneur's Toolkit Module on customer discovery here: https://toolkit.techstars.com/understand-your-customers.

My experience with customer discovery was pretty much face-to-face, doing the legwork from conference to conference, etc. My cofounders and I traveled to cleantech conferences and connected with local economic development agencies to find potential customers. Your university should be able to connect you to these types of opportunities if you're selling to another business. If you're selling to other consumers, your approach will be different from ours.

In the following story, Sam describes his experience with customer discovery and shares some great tips on how to build awareness of your product while you are still in college.

FEATURED STORY:
Sam Hollander,
CEO and Cofounder of
FSCL, Syracuse University,
Advertising and Finance
(Dual Degrees),
Graduated 2021

In the summer between freshman and sophomore year, looking at my finances and tuition bill for the upcoming school year, I realized I was facing a massive funding gap. I was trying to avoid accumulating more student debt, so I looked for alternatives. After months of research, I found multiple finance services for building a simpler, more affordable, and flexible solution to financing my education. I used this idea and my passion for and experience in entrepreneurship and finance to build my company, FSCL. Our vision was to transform students' lives by reducing financial stress, knowing that millions of students were going through the same financial issues as me.

At our most basic level, we are a financial intermediary. This means we have two business models: B2C (business to consumer) and B2B (business to business). I realized to make these business models work together, we needed to conduct extensive customer discovery to find that middle ground. Before we began to build our product, we needed to find the sweet spot wherein both consumers and businesses would use our products. We also needed to understand where we, as a company, fit strategically between our customers in both models.

I started simple, using the resources I had: friends and family. What started as friendly conversations turned into hour-long interviews and detailed questionaries. This process took months—seriously. For nine months, I did nothing but customer discovery. And customer discovery never ends; it's always ongoing.

THREE TAKEAWAYS FROM SAM:

1. A primary key to success in customer discovery is ensuring you are talking with as many people in your target market as possible. Everyone has their own viewpoint and lens they look at your business through. You need to hear all viewpoints so you can build an effective product.

2. Don't be afraid to follow up with questions and/or do another round of interviews. I've learned that hearing many different opinions leads to reimagining and rebuilding your product beyond your original idea. It's always good to keep in touch with your potential customers, and more often than not, they're happy to help. You can also keep these people in mind to be product testers.

3. Although customer discovery should be the first thing you do when you have an idea, it never ends. As you improve your product, continue to keep in touch with your customers and get feedback to continually make your product better.

#1 Lesson Learned: If I could only give one piece of advice to student-founders doing customer discovery, I'd say talk to as many people as you can. As I mentioned, everyone has their own background, experiences, and point of view, and listening to those different perspectives will yield a much better product.

About Sam: Sam is a Syracuse University senior studying finance and advertising, with an emphasis in financial and investor communications, graduating in December 2021. He's also the founder and CEO of FSCL, a company pioneering the use of alternative finance vehicles to build a more simple, affordable, and flexible solution to financing higher education. @samhollander

In the story below, Allen shares some tips for making connections when starting a new company as a young student. He emphasizes that students have a unique advantage and can leverage the university's network to get their company off the ground.

FEATURED STORY:
Allen Zhou,
Cofounder, Big & Mini, The University of Texas at Austin, Electrical and Computer Engineering, Graduating May 2023

In April 2020, I was finishing up my freshman year at the University of Texas at Austin, when suddenly, the pandemic hit, and our world changed. Loneliness ran rampant and millions (if not billions) around the world struggled with mental health issues. Seeing this, I wanted to help. I started by finding two of the smartest and hardest-working people I knew: my friend and peer at UT Austin, Aditi Merchant, and my brother Anthony, who was a senior in high school. I'd been mulling over a couple of ideas since COVID started and asked them what they thought of them.

Out of five ideas I proposed, only one resonated: creating meaningful, one-to-one connections between youths and older adults. That was the start of Big & Mini.

Once we picked the idea of connecting youths and seniors as our company's foundation, we decided to test the waters. We created a single-page website and a Google form. Then, we sent the form to our friends and family to see if anyone would try it out. A few did and we got our first dozen or so users.

With these first matches, we stumbled across a pivotal story that helped us understand the power of software to positively affect lives. After the first call with her Mini, the Big (the older adult) emailed us saying that the hour-long call with her Mini was "such a blast" and she "couldn't wait for the next one!" This brought us great joy and increased our enthusiasm for the mission, so we continued telling people.

We weren't sure where to go next. We'd exhausted our, our friends', and our families' connections. And, as teenagers with few other connections or experience, we had to create relationships from nothing—the cold email was our weapon. I personally emailed almost 100 faculty members, news outlets, organizations, and anyone who could help us. Even though many emails got no reply, a few did—which made it all worth it. We kept going, reaching out to individuals and groups around the nation.

Two weeks in, we reached a major milestone. Our outreach efforts helped us secure a feature in the *Houston Chronicle*, which led to many new sign-ups and greatly increased our credibility. We started developing our software, creating a login and sign-up system with integrated chat and calling capabilities, and writing a matching algorithm. Importantly, we didn't stop conducting out-reach efforts. We continued to update reporters and cold email organizations serving seniors. We started with Google, and the result was more connections made and loneliness combatted.

TOP TWO TAKEAWAYS:

1. Our hard work has started to pay off. Less than ten months in, we have thousands of Bigs and Minis from all fifty states and twenty-seven countries and have been featured in fifty-plus news outlets, including *The Today Show*, *Fox News*, and ABC. We've received funding from Techstars, Amazon, and Encore.org. We've even been described as "one of the most successful intergenerational programs in the last decade" by Professor Fingerman (our first cold email contact).

2. Big & Mini has been a testament to the power of sharing your story. But we've found it's not enough to create a brilliant piece of software. You have to continuously convince the world that what you have is worth their time. You have to tell the right people. And you have to be naively optimistic that you can change the world. Then you're well on your way to making billions of lives better.

#1 Lesson Learned: Creating a great product isn't enough. You have to continuously convince people that what you have is worth their time.

About Allen: Allen Zhou is a cofounder and CEO of Big & Mini, a platform that creates meaningful, one-to-one connections between youths and older adults. He's also an electrical and computer engineering major at the University of Texas at Austin and previously worked as a fellow at Norrsken VC, 8VC, and .406 Ventures.

PROTOTYPING BY DANIEL

Maybe you've worked out your business idea, talked to potential customers, and validated the need for your product. Now you need to build it. Whether your product is an app, some type of software, or a physical product, building it can be a daunting task. Perhaps you're an engineer and prototyping is right up your alley. But what if you're not? How do you find the right people to help you build your prototype? And more importantly, how do you pay for it?

In my experience, we were building a hardware product, so prototyping was both important and expensive. We found creative ways to fund our prototypes:

1. We leveraged (free) university labs and equipment.
2. We recruited students to help us (for free).
3. We raised any additional funds we needed through student pitch competitions and grants.

The next story, by Daniel, gives some great insights into how he built a prototype for his hardware product in college. Daniel leveraged the college of engineering on his campus and recruited engineers to help with his prototype. This option is a great way to keep costs down and account for any skill gaps you might have. Read Daniel's story for more.

FEATURED STORY:
Daniel Couser,
Founder and CEO, The
CALM Device, Temple
University, Bachelor of
Business Administration
- Entrepreneurship and
Innovation Management,
Graduated 2019

When I was growing up, I had a close friend who struggled with anxiety. Being close with this person, I was able to learn how disruptive anxiety can be. It can follow you to work, school, social settings, and everywhere else in between. I learned that there were many ways to help mitigate anxiety as a whole, like talk therapy, medications, and therapeutic devices, but there were not many ways to help de-escalate rising stress in the moment. While in college, I came across a research study titled "The Impact of Monaural Beat Stimulation on Anxiety and Cognition" that suggested pulses of sensory stimulation like sound or light could influence the brain and ultimately reduce stress. After discovering a few more supporting studies, I thought to myself, *Why couldn't this tech be put into something small, portable, and easy to use to help people deescalate rising stress in the moment?* I started talking to students, psychologists, and professors at my university to validate the concept, and after receiving very positive responses, I decided to start the company.

After validating the idea, I needed to build a proof-of-concept prototype to test my assumptions, but I had no idea where to start. I did not have an engineering background, and I had never soldered anything in my life. Building a prototype felt like an enormous task, but I knew that if I could clearly identify what I needed to build, I could figure out how to build it with some help.

Before building anything, I researched ways other successful startup founders had built their products. Listening to successful stories from other entrepreneurs can give you great insight into what went well, what to avoid, and how to best approach your prototype. After this initial research phase, it's a great idea to come up with specific questions and reach out to other startup founders who have built successful products to gain their insight and to build early connections with potential mentors.

Once I was ready to start scoping out the prototype, I began by defining what success looked like. This gave me a clear focus on the prototype's "need to haves" versus what was "nice to have." My first milestone was to build a functional proof-of-concept prototype that could generate one specific stimulation pattern and could test my assumptions. I laid out what I knew, what I needed to know, and the gap between the two. I needed to learn how to build the circuit, how to code a bare-bones version of the firmware, and how to create a basic enclosure. I started by searching tutorials online about how to build circuits and soon after headed to my university's engineering building to get hands-on experience. I connected with a few engineering students who helped answer my questions about circuitry and electrical engineering, giving me the knowledge I needed to build the prototype's circuit. After buying a few off-the-shelf electronic components, I created the first circuit and started to learn how to write very basic firmware. To learn, I used tutorials and documentation from Arduino, which is a great way to begin learning how to write firmware. (Arduino is a company that creates open-source hardware and software. With great tutorials on their website and a strong user community, Arduino can be a great starting point to learn about electronics.) With fewer than twenty lines of code, the first version of the electronics was finished. Finally, I needed to learn how to create the enclosure. After watching a few tutorials on 3D modeling, I headed to the engineering building once again and found a few students to help me learn the basics in 3D modeling software. With this help, I was able to create the first enclosure, use a 3D printer to create the housing, and finish the proof-of-concept prototype.

TOP THREE TAKEAWAYS:

1. Learning about how successful startup founders built their prototype is a great way to help navigate the challenges of developing your own prototype. Connecting with the right mentors early in the company's development is one of the most important things a startup founder can do.

2. Clearly define what success looks like and establish "the gap." Figure out what you know, what you need to know, and the gap between the two. This will help you identify the skills and information you and your team will need to hit your milestones.

3. As a student-founder, you have many resources, from other students, to on-campus resources, and especially, other entrepreneurs. These resources can help you build your prototype or even find a great cofounder in the process.

#1 Lesson Learned: One piece of advice I would give to a student-founder building a prototype is to connect with a great mentor who has successfully launched a product. Product development can be difficult, with many moving parts, and having someone who knows the challenges of your space firsthand to help guide you along the way is invaluable.

About Daniel: Daniel is a graduate of Temple University's Fox School of Business and the founder of Zen Stone. Daniel has brought the company through early validation, prototyping, and product development, and he is currently preparing Zen Stone to launch in consumer markets during the fourth quarter of 2021. He previously won first place in Temple University's Be Your Own Boss Bowl (undergraduate track, 2018) and brought Zen Stone through Techstars' Launchpad Lift program (2019).

PITCHING
BY KATARINA AND NICOLE

I f you've ever watched Shark Tank, you've seen a pitch. They really make pitching look easy on television, but reality is different. I found pitching particularly daunting because of my background. I was an engineer, and my first pitch was full of circuit diagrams, mathematical equations, and long paragraphs of text. It was a disaster. Thankfully, I learned there are proven formulas for mastering the pitch, including both pitch design and presentation.

In the first part of this chapter, we'll hear from Katarina. She's probably the most qualified student-founder to contribute to a chapter on pitching—ever. She's won twenty-two pitch/grant competitions, and even started another company to help other startup founders learn how to pitch. In her story, you'll learn some of her top tips for mastering pitches, keeping your equity, and funding a significant portion of your company.

FEATURED STORY:
Katarina Samardzija,
CEO and Founder,
Locker Lifestyle and
PowerToPitch, Grand
Valley State University,
Started with Biomedical
Sciences and Switched
to Entrepreneurship After
Starting Her Company,
Graduated 2019

It all started one day after tennis practice when my team-mates and I went to the gym. All we needed was an ID and key, but we ended up bringing bulky wallets. When we had our valuables stolen out of the open gym cubbies, I *knew* I had to do something about it because the only alternative was bulky, poor-quality running belts. Fortunately, my "momager," as I like to call my friend who has kids, had a bridal store. At the end of 2016, I met with her seamstress to devise a solution for storing our valuables. Locker Lifestyle was founded to help people feel confident about where they're going and what they're doing. We create wearable wrist wallets and pocket neck gaiters to secure IDs, keys, and phones for fitness, travel, shopping, festivals, and more. I started selling products out of my dorm room, and everyone was asking where they could get one!

Unfortunately, shortly after starting the business, it came to a devastating halt. My mother's store burned to the ground, which also meant I lost all my materials, patterns, and prototypes. I was back to zero, but I knew if I could sell out of product without marketing, I had to find a way to get back in business. In 2017, I entered my first pitch competition and won $7,500 to build my website and invest in my first large-scale manufacturing batch. I was back and better than ever.

The cash from my first pitch win went fast. I was still training for tennis, maintaining dean's list status, and running the business. I saw a future in my brand and I became obsessed with it, so I knew I needed to protect what I was building. To fund the business, I entered another pitch competition—then another, then another—and in 2020, I won my twenty-second grant, while maintaining 100 percent ownership in Locker Lifestyle. In 2018, I was the youngest person to win the FedEx Small Business Grant. They brought a production team to my home to film me talking about the strategies I used to enter and win their competition. The interview went viral, and I received hundreds of messages from entrepreneurs around the country asking for pitch advice.

Since I couldn't respond to everyone individually, I created my second company, PowerToPitch.com, to educate, inspire, and help small business owners find and win grants. My first workshop was such an incredible success that I now serve on multiple boards and create custom workshops for organizations like Draper University. I realized there was a lack of available and affordable resources for teaching individuals and small business owners how to present themselves and find funding to grow their company. I am on a mission to give individuals and businesses the power to *pitch* themselves to success.

TOP THREE TAKEAWAYS:

1. Start with your story. Many entrepreneurs make the mistake of starting with what they do. This should come last. *Always* start with your "why," your motivation, your passion, and how your business idea came about—this is why people will invest in your business. It will help them choose *you* first.

2. Procrastination will hurt future opportunities. When looking for grants, I recommend looking one whole year ahead and figuring out a schedule of when items are due, what you will need, and what the criteria is. If you think you can fill out a whole application and make a pitch video hours before it's due, your odds of winning are slim.

3. Quality is everything. Everyone you meet is an opportunity to practice your pitch. Your messaging is constantly evolving and takes lots of practice. You never know whom you might be pitching to or if they can even help you with your business!

#1 Lesson Learned: Persistence and passion are the ingredients to success. I was only nineteen when I started my first company, so a lot of suppliers took advantage of me. I had no idea I could negotiate pricing and materials, and many future retail partners didn't take me seriously. I kept asking for feedback so they couldn't ignore me. When I pitched Locker Life-style to get on *Good Morning America* three times, the suppliers were begging to have my products instead of me begging them! Try and try again; persistence will get you a yes. Passion will get you what you want.

About Kat: Kat started her first business, Locker Lifestyle, in college after being a victim of theft. She funded the business by winning twenty-two entrepreneurship competitions (including being the youngest person to win the FedEx grant contest). After getting thousands of messages asking how she won competitions, she created her second company, PowerToPitch, to coach individuals and businesses on effectively telling their stories. Read more here: www.PowerToPitch.com.

Next, you're in for a treat. I've included lessons from someone who might possibly be the best pitch coach in the world—Nicole Glaros, chief investment strategy officer at Techstars. Oh, and if you'd like to read more, Nicole has done a great overview of this topic in the Techstars' Toolkit Modules here:

Give Your Elevator Pitch:

https://toolkit.techstars.com/give-your-elevator-pitch

Master Your Pitch:

https://toolkit.techstars.com/master-your-pitch

**HOW TO PITCH
by Nicole Glaros,**
Chief Investment
Strategy Officer at
Techstars

So you've got a business idea. Congratulations! There is nothing more fun and rewarding, or brutal and thankless, than trying to bring your idea to life. One of the first things you need to learn is how to communicate that idea in a way others will understand. If you cannot do this one deceptively complex task, you'll never find employees, customers, partners, or capital to help your business.

So where do you start? This quick outline will help you understand how to develop a framework for building an excellent pitch. Please note there is an exhaustive number of high-quality resources on the subject of developing an excellent pitch—and this chapter is by no means an in-depth analysis. It does, however, get you off on the right foot, and I highly suggest you check out some books and videos to help you on your journey.

Always start with the goal

If you want to pitch the idea, what's the goal? *Why* are you pitching? Likely each time you pitch, you might have a different goal in mind. It can save you an incredible amount of time to articulate the goal behind each pitch because each goal might emphasize different elements of your business. For instance, are you pitching to a friend you want to join you as a cofounder? Are you pitching to an engineering firm to get them to help you build the product? Are you pitching to investors to raise capital? Are you in a pitch competition where the audience is general and you need to appeal to the most common denominator? This chapter focuses on a goal of raising capital, but having other goals is also acceptable. Simply write them down to articulate them and you'll be much more likely to achieve your goal.

Know your audience

Understanding a pitch happens at the listener's ears, not at the presenter's mouth. That means you need to tailor your presentation to each audience, understanding what excites them, understanding what motivates them, and explaining why they should listen or care. It's very common to have different versions of a pitch depending on whom you're presenting to. Ensuring that every sentence you utter leverages their interests will propel your pitch, and thus your business, forward.

This chapter is oriented around an investor pitch, specifically when you're talking to angel investors or seed-stage venture capitalists and looking to raise equity capital for your business. At the end of the day, investors are looking for returns, so they are evaluating the business' scale and likelihood of success, whereas a customer pitch tends to evaluate the product more. Understanding the difference between an investor pitch and a customer pitch is important. Remember that investors want to understand how they will make a return, in what time frame, and in what multiple.

The sections of your investor pitch

Your pitch has nine sections, not including the opening logo slide and the closing logo/contact info slide, and each section should have a corresponding slide (or two) in a presentation deck. Many investors want you to email the deck prior to agreeing to a meeting, so your pitch deck is more than a tool to aid you in your presentation; it's a door opener when done right. Investors get hundreds, sometimes thousands, of pitch decks every year, and the default behavior is to skim them. Including these sections will ensure you have the right ingredients for speaking to the equity investor in a culture that skims content. Here's a brief outline of the sections:

Logo slide with your name/email address.

1. The intro with problem or opportunity
2. The solution with product demo
3. The market size
4. Customer acquisition strategy
5. The business model
6. The differentiation
7. Traction
8. Team
9. Ask

Logo slide with your name/email address

The more concise the deck, the more powerful and effective it will be to get a meeting. A deck with fifteen or less slides is a good guideline—something the investors can flip through quickly to get the gist of what you will present. It's best to leave out certain information (like financials or the specific details on how the technology might work) because it makes a deck significantly longer and it's confidential information that's better discussed live than in a document that can be emailed outside of your control. Also, note that the section requirements might change depending on your audience; for instance, if you're pitching to a room full of scientists, you might want to go heavier on the specific details of the invention, or if you're pitching to a room full of potential customers, you will likely want to omit the business model and market size slides. If you're pitching to a banker, you will likely have to include actual historical financials. "Know your audience!"

The intro

This section and the corresponding slides have four goals: introduce yourself, establish baseline credibility (if possible), succinctly and powerfully state the problem or opportunity you're tackling, and capture the listener's attention and imagination. The trick is doing this in less than thirty seconds, and you increase your likelihood of success here if you do it faster. If you don't capture their attention in the first thirty seconds or so, they won't hear anything else you say. I tend to get a lot of pushback on this timing—but I want you to think for a moment about the last time you sat through a video ad or commercial and paid rapt attention the whole way through. It is likely your attention dropped off after the first five to ten seconds and never really came back, and unfortunately for you, the same thing will happen with your audience unless you can really capture their imagination and interest quickly. Still don't believe me? Attend a local pitch competition, and rather than watching the presenters, watch the audience. See how long it takes them to check out. It's terrifying.

Okay, how do you capture their "rapt" attention? It's really hard to do and will take a lot of iterations to get it right, but here are some ideas to get you started:

- Tell a personal story (in less than fifteen seconds). Of all the possibilities, what motivated you to start this particular company?

- Make me laugh.

- Contradict conventional wisdom.

- Play on a fear.

- Tell me a startling fact.

- Be different.

The solution/product—aka, the demo section

This section and the corresponding slides simply and visually demonstrate the solution to the problem or opportunity you highlighted in the previous section. The shortcut to making this section powerful is to avoid *describing* your product or solution, but use visuals to *show* it. Words alone can sink you here, but words along with a visual demonstration will help you stand apart. Screenshots or a video walkthrough can work wonders—and you get bonus points if you highlight in your demo the things that make your business unique (for instance the business model or certain killer features that will set you apart from your competition). Where most startup founders get this wrong is they use too many words and not enough visuals to show the solution. This is crucial because as investors, we listen to hundreds if not thousands of pitches a year. I guarantee they've heard your idea before, so if you use only words to describe it, it will sound like all the other similar ideas, and it will immediately be dismissed as *uninteresting.* Using images will help investors see the product through your eyes and will help them understand what makes it different than anything else they've seen.

The market size

After decades of doing this, my favorite suggestion for handling market size is to discuss your total addressable market (TAM), or your best guess, and how much revenue your company could generate annually given the total number of customers and the cost of your product if it owned 100 percent of the market. For instance (a super-simplistic example), if you're selling a new kind of disposable diaper and there are 2 million babies born each year in the US, and each baby uses about five diapers a day each year, and you'll charge about $0.15 per diaper, your total addressable market is 2 million x 5 x 365 x 0.15 = $547,500,000 annually in the US alone, not including babies who use diapers for more than a year. As an investor, I'm going to take that number and say, "Okay, what percent of the market does the largest competitor own?" Let's say it's 5 percent which means $547,500,000 x 0.05 = $27,375,000 per year in annual topline revenue. This number helps both me and you understand if we're a good fit. As a larger venture capitalist, this number might be too small to be interesting. As a seed venture fund, it might be good. As an angel investor, I might love this number. Contrast this with a dry cleaner. Let's say you want to open a dry cleaners and believe it will attract business in a two-mile radius. Assuming there are 5,000 households in that two-mile radius, and each household will launder roughly five items a year, and the average cost per item is $15, you're looking at a TAM of 5,000 x 5 x $15 = $375,000 annually, and that's without looking at how much competition might be in the area.

The big takeaway here is to really focus on what your addressable market is—not some other number. If you're selling diapers, don't come at me saying the US spends $500 billion on babies each year, unless you're also prepared to tell me about how you're going to move into different products in the same market. Or if you're in the dry-cleaning business, don't tell me what people spend in the US on dry cleaning; your information needs to be hyper-local unless you're starting some global mail-in dry cleaning service. Most startup founders put some huge number up on the screen because they've heard that investors want to see big numbers. While this is true, if you present a number that doesn't represent what you're actually chasing, it makes the investor think you don't know what you're talking about and disbelieve other numbers in your presentation. In my humble opinion, err on the side of accuracy rather than using bombastic descriptions because you risk attracting investors who also enjoy bombastic language in their definitions of how they'll treat you and value your business.

Customer acquisition strategy

I love it when startup founders put this slide in their presentation because it shows they've given it some serious thought. Yes, I know you will advertise, and you know you will advertise. The question is how and to whom, and how much is it going to cost you (CAC or customer acquisition cost). Telling me you're going to advertise on Facebook is good. Telling me you're advertising on Facebook and you get roughly a 1 percent clickthrough rate and then a 1 percent conversion rate (fairly standard by the way), but you also have a channel partnership with these other retailers and have put together a referral program and three other channel strategies tells me you're actually working on sales.

The business model

The business model is the rough economic model of the business. If you're selling software as a service, is it a subscription or one-time purchase? How much? If it's a product you're producing, what is the cost to produce it, and what will you charge for it? What are the high-level costs of goods sold (COGS) of the business? As an investor, I need to understand the company's economic engine or I won't be able to assess what my own returns from the investment might be.

Differentiation

Most startups like to include their competition—but what I want to know is how you are going to beat your competition. Of course, it's important for you to know who they are, but take it one step farther and tell me why customers are going to choose your product over that of your competitors. This subtle nuance can be powerful in getting investors to see the real opportunity you're presenting.

Traction

Showing market traction just means showing evidence that the market is actually buying or using your product. Great traction slides include how much revenue, how many users or customers, or how many signups you have. Also, putting this information on a timeline chart helps me understand how quickly you are growing. One-hundred users might not be an impressive number, but if you tell me you got them in the last fifteen minutes, that's more interesting. Often with investors, it's not the ultimate number, but rather the shape of the growth chart that's more interesting. Also, traction numbers show me the business isn't just an idea for you—you've actually started the business.

Team

What makes you uniquely qualified to build this company, how do you know your cofounders, and what advisors have you assembled to help guide you on this journey? I was once on the board of a company where the founder was the CEO and he was building his first company producing restaurant software. He had a great background because he was the third generation of his family to own a famous restaurant in a large city, and as a college student, he helped his family's restaurant by implementing new software systems, so he knew the pain of bringing technology to a largely analog industry intimately. Once he started the company, he assembled a team of advisors and board members who either came from the restaurant software or restaurant operations industries, thereby surrounding himself with experts in the field. If you or your cofounders don't have a unique background in the industry, make sure you find advisors or mentors who can help guide you along the journey.

Ask

When you're talking to investors, your "ask" is your fundraising target. For instance, "We're raising $2.5 million. We already have $750,000 committed, and I'd love to know if you find this investment opportunity interesting enough to schedule another meeting with me to dive deeper into our technology." However, not all pitches are to investors, so always take a moment to make an ask. Whether it's asking for feedback on your product, letting them know you're looking for a new vice president of engineering and would love some introductions, or maybe you're looking for a Facebook video marketing expert, always take advantage of the opportunity to ask for help. A quick note—if you're raising money, you can run afoul of the SEC (U.S. Securities and Exchange Commission) and rack up serious fines and fees by inadvertently engaging in "general solicitation," which means asking an unknown group of people for capital. In the US, don't stand up in front of a group of people and fundraise unless you have your attorney's permission.

Some pro-tips

People can either listen or read; they cannot do both simultaneously. What that means is to be thoughtful about how many words you put on each slide. If you're talking to someone, you want the slides to have images that reinforce what you're saying; otherwise, investors are going to read the slide and not listen to you. But if you email someone a presentation without enough words, they won't understand what you're trying to convey. Conversely, if you email someone a presentation that has too many words, they won't read it anyway. (Remember, investors usually skim.) Seek balance in the number of words versus visuals on a screen—I say no more than five to seven words on a screen if you're talking through it, and no more than ten to twelve words on a screen if you're emailing it.

Don't use animation—we are adults, and most of us stopped watching cartoons a long time ago. Animation today feels lazy to the investor. Spend the time making screen shots of your product or pay a designer to build a graphic representation of what it should look like. Slide animations are distracting and annoying.

Iterate! Start off with three or four different versions of your pitch (which will help keep you from being too committed to one version that may not actually work that well), and present those options to others to see where you get the most positive and negative reactions. Ask people where their minds wandered. Ask people what they disbelieved. Ask people what resonated with them and what didn't. The more feedback you get here, the better. Then take that feedback and build in improvements or consider starting from scratch if necessary. Someone telling you that you did a good job is not constructive. You need to figure out what to improve if you're going to be successful. In fact, if all you hear is "Good job," find different people who will give you honest assessments. Try to identify people who will think similarly to the investors you'll eventually be pitching. You're not likely to get great feedback from your mom, even if she is well intentioned, unless she's an investor.

Simplify, simplify, simplify. Some of the most powerful stories and presentations I've seen have been the simplest ones, and some of the least effective have been the most complicated. Ruthlessly cut content to simplify, and use conversations with the investor to help explain what you cut out. You don't need to put everything in a presentation.

Follow-up and follow-through. The pitch is only a third of the effort in raising capital. You also need to identify the right investors and get them to say yes. Make sure you're following up with every person you meet with, and ensure you do what you say you're going to do. If you tell an investor you're going to get back to them next week and you fail to do so, they assume that's how you'll act as the CEO of your business (and they're probably right). Always send follow-up emails, always have a next step, and do what you say you're going to do. I've made investments in companies where I didn't love the product or the market, but I ended up investing simply because the founder always did what they said they were going to do—and that eventually leads to success.

Find your tribe. Starting a company is one of the toughest things you'll ever do, next to raising kids. While you can do it alone, your odds of success plummet without support. Find other startup founders in a similar stage as you and in stages one or two steps ahead of where you are. Lean on each other for support, always help others in areas where they struggle, and know that wave of support will one day lift you up and carry you forward in ways unimaginable today. If you can't find that tribe, build it.

> **About Nicole:** Nicole has been investing in and mentoring startup founders for nearly twenty years. Currently, Nicole is the chief investment strategy officer at Techstars, where she aided the company's meteoric growth from ten companies in the portfolio to more than 2,500 and helped raise the Techstars' $150 million venture fund. Additionally, she works closely with founders to help maximize their performance, thereby helping their companies achieve their potential. Nicole is on the board of directors for the National Venture Capital Association, the Federal Reserve Bank of Kansas City, Denver Branch, and has held board positions at Pana, Ordermark, Greathorn, and others.

FUNDRAISING BY CODY AND MATT

This might be the chapter you've been waiting for. Maybe you even skipped the rest of the chapters just to read this one. (Shame on you!) Either way, "How do I raise funds as a student?" is a question I hear a lot. With a limited network and limited experience, you might be wondering how to find funding, what types of groups will work with students, and how to prepare for those opportunities. For me, we entered every pitch competition we could, applied for state and national government grants, and attempted to raise venture capital (VC) funding. It was an incredible learning experience, and I only wish I'd had the advice Cody gives below when I was going through the process myself.

I wanted to cover the bases in this chapter, so I asked a former colleague of mine, Cody Simms, partner at My Climate Journey and previously senior vice president at Techstars, to help out.

FUNDRAISING
by Cody Simms,
Partner at My Climate
Journey

At a time when many of your peers are simply trying to figure out how to fund doing their laundry this week, you are trying to capitalize your startup business. First, let me start by congratulating you on your drive and vision. Rather than thinking about the job you'll try to get after you graduate, you are thinking about the future you are creating for yourself, and hopefully, for many others. I was not entrepreneur-minded like you in college; most people are not. However, even though I am more than two decades removed from college, I've spent the last year cofounding a climate action non-profit (climatechangemakers.org) with a college undergraduate. I've seen firsthand just how incredible college-aged startup founders can be.

There is a difference, however, between building a great product and getting funding for it as a company. Building a product is really hard, but if you have unique insight on a customer need and you are great at listening to your customers and executing product development, you can catch lightning in a bottle somewhat on your own. Getting people, often strangers, to part with their hard-earned dollars to fund your vision of the future is an entirely different skill. That said, here are a few key steps you can take to help demystify the fundraising process—there are even a few places where you have a distinct advantage as a student.

Step 1: Ignore the noise

This is really hard to do, but the first step I suggest is to ignore what you see in the news on TechCrunch, Twitter, Crunchbase, The Verge, etc. about funding. It's really easy to get caught up in the hype-cycle of how much money some other company raised and at what valuation. There are a few important things to keep in mind: 1) what you are seeing in the news is the end of the fundraising cycle after all negotiations have happened, 2) unsuccessful rounds (of which there are countless) don't get announced, and 3) you don't know what investor relationships the founders of any of these companies had at the start. Step one is to ignore the noise and focus on the variables you can control.

Step 2: Hard conversations and structures

Do you have a cofounder? Have you formally decided on roles? Have you discussed—and I mean really discussed—who among you is the CEO and why? Have you formally decided on equity splits? I mean, have you really discussed it rather than just defaulting to a fifty-fifty split? Are you sure you are all 100 percent comfortable with everything you will be doing together and who will do what? Have you incorporated the company? Or if not but you plan to, have you already sorted out what that's going to look like and cost? Do you have a lawyer? My general advice is that if you haven't already incorporated, maybe save yourself the legal expense and wait until your fundraising is making progress, but have everything 100 percent ready to go, which includes having had the hard conversations about roles and compensation. You don't want to wait until after you've raised money to find out that you disagree fully on equity percentages between the founders.

Step 3: Get organized

As a student-founder, investors will likely assume you are less organized and professional than a typical startup founder. This is unfair and is an implicit bias on their part. Your job is to take advantage of that bias by being the most organized startup founder they've ever met. When you do this, you will impress them five times more than a typical founder would. (This implicit bias is to your advantage as long as you take advantage of it.) Being organized means having what I call your fundraising "*mise en place*" ready to go before you start fundraising. *Mise en place* is a French culinary phrase that means the chef has all of the ingredients measured and prepped before they begin cooking. Similarly, you should have your fundraising materials ready to go before you begin fundraising. If you have all of this stuff ready, you will come across as being in the top 5 percent of most prepared founders, which will help you come across as a real professional when you meet with investors. The "Build an Investor Pipeline" workshop series on the Techstars Entrepreneur's Toolkit (https://toolkit.techstars.com/) outlines the key elements of your investor *mise en place* but, in short, it should include:

- **Investor pipeline:** A lightweight list of investor targets you can share with key mentors and allies.

- **Process starter email:** This is the email you'll use to personally engage key mentors in your process.

- **Investor CRM:** CRM stands for customer relationship management. This is a software platform you'll use to manage your fundraising process and interactions.

- **Forwardable email draft:** This email will be forwarded by mentors/contacts to investors. This is the email you send when you are actually ready to get in front of an investor, and your contact will forward it on your behalf.

- **One-pager (optional):** This is a quick snapshot of your company, traction, and other insight that could be helpful to an investor.

- **Pitch deck:** Have one version of your presentation ready with any sensitive information removed in case you need to email it.

- **Financial model:** With a well-built financial model, you can have a deeper conversation about the assumptions you have of your business. It will help you show that you've really thought through the things that drive your business. Just this one step alone will set you apart from 97 percent of other pre-seed and seed stage companies.

- **Cap table:** Make sure your cap table (a spreadsheet or table showing the capitalization equity for your company) is up-to-date before you begin to fundraise. The last thing you want is to get to the finish line and then have a round held up due to cap table issues.

- **Data room:** Your data room is a shared drive (e.g., Dropbox or Box.com) that has access controls and includes most of the key documents above, such as your presentation, financial model, cap table, and other materials you want to share with investors who are deep into due diligence.

Step 4: Know what you don't know and be humble about it

One of the fallacies of raising capital is assuming that you need to show you have everything figured out. Guess what? You are an early-stage startup; you have very little figured out. The best startup founders know this and use it to their advantage. Rather than trying to give detailed answers to every investor question, know that it's okay if the answer is, "We don't know that yet." Ideally, follow up with, "And here is our plan to figure it out. This is one of our key unvalidated assumptions." To that end, knowing what your top unvalidated assumptions are—which as an early startup really should be a list of the most important things you need to figure out next, and in what order you plan to try to validate those things—is gold. Here's an example: an investor asks you, "Okay, so you are targeting developers as customers. Is your focus more on independent developers or engineering managers at small and mid-size companies?" Now, you could be tempted to answer with what you think the answer should be, but if you don't actually know which will convert better, you'd be better off saying something akin to, "We don't know yet. We know that, generally, developers love our product as evidenced by the retention rate we have to date, and we feel great about that. But we don't yet know which segments of the developer market to target. Our assumption is that we should start by targeting indie developers and then go upstream since we've seen many successful companies follow that path, but as part of the use of funds from this round, we plan to do some targeting experiments to validate this assumption." This is a humble way to admit what you don't know while also looking super on top of things.

Step 5: Negotiation is not your friend

You are a team of three college kids who have not raised money before, and you've got your first pitch meeting lined up with an angel investor. Within the first three minutes, the investor asks, "So what sort of funding round are you putting together? How much are you raising, and do you have terms?" How do you answer? If you didn't take my advice in Step 1 above, you may be tempted to be bigger than your britches and try to sound like one of the startups on TechCrunch by saying, "We're raising X on Y valuation." *Do not do this!* Why not? Because at this moment, you have zero leverage. The investor can easily just start negotiating numbers with you, and they hold all of the cards because you want their money and they have no urgency. Instead, a better response is to be humble and say, "We don't know yet. We're just starting to talk to investors, and as part of that, we're trying to get a sense of the market." Most investors will totally get this. If they insist on getting to the nitty-gritty details, try something like, "Honestly, we don't know yet. This is our first funding round, so we're thinking it will be a round size of roughly X, but we certainly don't know the valuation because we want to see what the market will bear." Then, if you want to be extra-savvy, you can say, "Based on what you've heard from us, what do you think our funding target should be this round, and do you have a sense of valuation?" Do this often and you'll get some real data about how the market values what you are building. You can also add an awesome follow-up question, which is, "So, if we were to raise roughly that amount at that valuation, is that something you'd be interested in exploring with us?" And the last thing you'd want to ask is, "What, if anything, have you heard today that causes you concern?" The key takeaway here is that you'll fundraise most successfully by using your ears and not your mouth. You don't have leverage to command a deal, so don't act as though you do. But if you ask questions and collect data, you'll really learn a lot that will make each investor conversation that much more productive.

This section on fundraising could easily be a book by itself; hopefully, you found some key takeaways such as be organized, don't try to be what you are not, and view each interaction as a learning experience rather than a sales experience. Good luck, and use the possibility of people underestimating you to your advantage!

About Cody: Cody Simms is a Partner with My Climate Journey—a climate community, media creator, and climate tech venture fund. He is also co-founder of Climate Changemakers, a 501(c)(4) climate-focused political action network, and co-author of the Amazon-bestselling book *Levers: The Framework for Building Repeatability into Your Business* (leversbook.com). Cody previously served as Senior Vice President of Climate & Sustainability at Techstars and as an investing Partner in Techstars' institutional venture funds. He is also the host of the Techstars Climate Tech Podcast. Cody joined Techstars in 2013 as the first Managing Director in Los Angeles while establishing the Disney Accelerator powered by Techstars and co-investing with Disney in twenty startups from 2014-15.

Now that you have some expert advice on fundraising, we'll finish this chapter by sharing Matt's perspective as a student-founder. Matt offers tips on how to prepare to fundraise and how to find the right connections.

FEATURED STORY: Matt Shumer, Cofounder and CEO, OthersideAI, Syracuse University, Entrepreneurship, Dropped Out to Work On His Startup

When I got to college in 2018, I started a medical virtual reality hardware company called Visos. It gained traction quickly, and in the year and a half after founding, we had made significant progress and formed partnerships with some of the largest companies in tech. However, in early 2020, COVID hit, and we soon found that the market was no longer able to support medical VR solutions like Visos. At the time, I had been very interested in language technology, and I had built an in-house product to help Miles (cofounder) and I write email faster using artificial intelligence. After the market shift, we decided to go all-in and focus on the email product. Since then, we've been building OthersideAI, which allows users to write a simple summary of what they want to say, and our AI (artificial intelligence) turns that into a full, well-written email message.

As a college student looking to raise capital for my startup, I ran into a number of challenges. And since I was not at a top-tier school, those challenges were magnified significantly. On top of that, it was nearly impossible to figure out how to raise funds, which investors to talk to, and how to connect with them.

I started by pitching in university competitions and perfecting my narrative. After I had the basics of pitching down, I reached out to a few people in the AI community for advice. When I was ready to start looking for funding, these people graciously offered to connect me with investors they thought would be great partners for Otherside. Those connections allowed us to raise enough capital to get started, and the initial investors who put money in put us in touch with larger funds, which helped us in our seed round. Focus was imperative here—I made sure only to connect with investors who were great fits for Otherside. At my last startup, I wasted a lot of time talking to investors who were outside of my industry or didn't invest in the development stage I was fundraising for, and I wasn't able to raise capital because of it.

TOP THREE TAKEAWAYS:

1. Perfect your pitch as much as possible before meeting investors, and view your first few investor pitches as practice pitches. After every pitch, take the feedback you get and incorporate it into your narrative for the next time you pitch.

2. Use Crunchbase to look into investors before meeting with them. If they don't invest in your industry/stage, they likely won't invest. If they're not a fit, don't spend time meeting with them.

3. Create urgency—I spent way too much time saying I was raising without a deadline, and this led to very little investor interest; without a deadline, investors will wait to commit until other investors have invested. It's uncomfortable to do at first, but saying, "We're closing this round in two weeks," forces investors to decide quickly. Your chance of success increases significantly with a deadline.

#1 Lesson Learned: Raising capital is insanely difficult (sometimes it feels nearly impossible), but if you have a great pitch and vision, and drive urgency, you can raise a round of funding from amazing investors. And if you don't get it right the first time, you can always try again. I tried to fundraise a few times before I cashed my first checks—it's rare for an entrepreneur to close a round of fundraising on the first try.

About Matt: Matt is the cofounder and CEO of OthersideAI, which creates cutting-edge AI-powered communications tools. Previously, Matt founded Visos, a startup developing next-generation virtual reality software designed for medical use, and FURI, a company aiming to democratize access to sporting goods by creating high-performance products and selling them for fair prices.

LEGAL STUFF BY BREEZY

It might be the last thing you're thinking about as a new founder, but finding good legal help early on with your startup is an important step in ensuring your company is set up for success. When I started my company in college, I was fortunate enough to get connected to the legal clinic on campus. Many universities have these. As a student, you can often get free or heavily discounted legal services from these clinics. The clinic on my campus helped us with writing our operating agreement (very important if you have cofounders) and provided guidance with trademarks and patents. I highly recommend asking around to see if you have a clinic on your campus. When it comes to legal, unless you have a law degree, you are probably not aware of all the things you should do to avoid headaches in the future.

In the story that follows, Breezy shares her experience with a trademark issue and provides some tips on how to avoid the situation she found herself in.

FEATURED STORY:
Breezy Baldwin,
CEO, Hovr, University
of Central Florida,
Computer Science,
Didn't Graduate

Note: Breezy is sharing her personal story and experience finding legal help. She is not providing legal advice in any official sense.

Before returning to school when I was twenty-eight, I backpacked and lived in Europe, where I frequently used a long-distance carpooling app to get around. In Europe, there are 70 million active users on long-distance carpooling applications. Europeans embraced this communal road-tripping years ago—in part due to higher gas prices, but also due to a more open mindset to "strangers" and an earlier commitment to reducing carbon emissions. I was super-frustrated when I returned to the US to find there was no similar app here, so I set out to create it. I knew going back to school would not only help me learn the skills necessary to create an app and a company, but the startup programs would provide invaluable resources.

After my company had been in business for more than a year, we got a trademark infringement letter, demanding we rebrand within a set, short timeframe or be sued for damages. Until it happens to you, getting hit with a legal issue is something you don't realize can destroy your business—especially a young student startup. It was completely unexpected, and it drained our financial resources and ten months of our time, putting a halt to any real progress for the company.

At my university, I was fortunate enough to have an amazing startup program (Upstarts), a Blackstone LaunchPad, and dozens of mentors found through these resources. The city my school is in (Orlando) also had an incredible city-sponsored startup program (Starter Studio). I had a low-cost LegalZoom subscription. I consulted friends who were lawyers and many business owners. Law is extremely nuanced and complex, so the advice I got from almost everyone was either to hire a lawyer or give in entirely. I decided it wasn't in our best interest to spend what amounted to way more than our total cash reserves to hire a lawyer. Instead, I spent dozens of hours teaching myself about trademark law using abundant free resources online. I was able to figure out on my own that we did have a fighting chance. After months of back-and-forth with the opposing lawyers, we came to a settlement that was fair for all and were able to move forward with our venture.

TOP THREE TAKEAWAYS:

1. Law and legal issues can seem super-scary, and most people will tell you to leave it to the experts (which is probably what you should do), but don't be afraid to do legal research on your own and question the advice you are getting. How much you can learn may surprise you. I found the most helpful advice was often on the blogs of lawyers who were highly specialized in the exact problem I had. Declassified documents from past lawsuits were also very helpful—a Beyoncé lawsuit I found helped a lot.

2. LegalZoom and similar low-cost legal services can give you peace of mind for a lot of things, but I found when it came to actually facing a major legal issue, all the normal (very expensive) fees applied.

3.

Before paying precious startup cash for a lawyer, ask everyone you know if they have any friends who are lawyers who may be willing to give pro bono counsel. After posting to Facebook about my legal issues, a few people connected me to their lawyers. Unfortunately, none specialized in trademark law, but many would have been willing to help out.

#1 Lesson Learned: Our legal troubles actually came about from not initially paying just a few hundred dollars for a lawyer to file our trademark. Don't be lazy about trademarking! The second you have a name picked out, hire a lawyer to do due diligence and trademark it for you. This could protect you from facing huge legal issues in the future. This same principle can apply to all potential legal issues. Regularly check to see if there is anything you could get into trouble for legally. That way a lot of legal problems can be easily prevented.

About Breezy: Over the past fifteen years, Breezy has been a CEO, COO, creative director, developer, designer, photographer, and videographer. She's been to forty-seven countries and all fifty US states and became an early ambassador for the sharing economy and sustainable travel. She loves to surf, scuba dive, and snowboard.

PATENTS BY MARCO

Disclaimer: I'm not a patent attorney, nor is the contributor to this chapter. I suggest you seek legal counsel from your university or elsewhere before making a major decision about patents.

A question I get a lot from early-stage startup founders is: Should I patent my product? Whoa. That's a loaded question. Many factors need to be considered when thinking about a patent. From my personal experience, the patent process can be long, expensive, and doesn't necessarily protect you from your competition (unless you're ready to lawyer-up in a most expensive way). Recently, I've seen fewer startups talking about patenting than ever before. This may be because, regardless of whether you patent, the success of your startup depends more heavily on your ability to *execute* and sell your product faster and better than anyone else. Those factors are independent of a patent.

Of course, some fields may require patents, such as the medical field. Or in the case of my company, we knew we were working with a technology that could be licensed to a much larger company, so we chose to patent our technology. We chose to (1) license a patent from the university we attended, and (2) develop our own technology outside the university and patent it on our own. The former took a long time—more than a year to obtain a license agreement. The latter was expensive. We spent well over $100,000 on the process, including legal fees. But each university is different, and some universities are very advanced with their patent process. As you'll see in Marco's story in this chapter, working with his university's intellectual property (IP) office was good for their team.

Deciding if you should patent is a conversation you should have with a trusted mentor. In this chapter, we focus on a story from a student-founder who decided to patent. Marco shares his experiences as a doctoral student—from taking an entrepreneurship class to meeting cofounders and working with his university's IP office. He'll offer some key takeaways and considerations for if you go down the patent path.

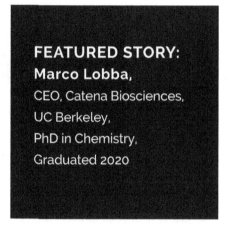

FEATURED STORY:
Marco Lobba,
CEO, Catena Biosciences,
UC Berkeley,
PhD in Chemistry,
Graduated 2020

When I was halfway into my five-year doctoral program in chemistry, I found that my primary research project was completely non-viable and had to be abandoned. I was very fortunate to have begun working to help another graduate student on their project where we happened to notice an unexpected product every time we ran the reaction. After further experiments and validation, we determined that we had discovered an exciting technology capable of attaching whole proteins together! This technique would be useful to many industries but was most relevant to developing new types of therapeutics. With no idea how to start a business, I decided to take an entrepreneurship class at the Haas MBA program, which is where I ended up meeting my cofounder Geo and launching Catena. Since then, we've been pushing forward with our dream to create cures for autoimmune disease and other conditions using this amazing protein attachment technology.

We knew from day one that our discovery in lab had the potential to benefit not just therapeutic development, but could also have applications in everything from diagnostic tests to making better cleaning products. However, as academics, we needed to publish our results to have other scientists validate our experiment and ensure the technology could be used by as many people as possible. The challenge is that anything you publish in a paper or present at a conference becomes public knowledge, and therefore, not something that can be protected by a patent. Given the high economic potential of our discovery, we knew we would need to have some protections in place before we could publish our paper on the technology.

Thankfully, I had been to several presentations given by Berkeley's intellectual property office (IPIRA) which talked about the process of filing a patent through them. Since our technology was discovered at Berkeley using campus resources and federal funding, it was our opportunity and duty to discuss the technology's potential with them to decide if filing a patent was the right decision. After a short initial meeting, it was clear that the technology had enough potential to justify the patent process. We were put in contact with a patent attorney who helped turn our five-page manuscript draft into a 100-page patent application in just a few short weeks. Since the university owns the rights to technology developed in its facilities, we, as inventors, did not have to pay any of the legal fees associated with this process. As a student interested in commercializing this technology, I then could go back to Berkeley and negotiate a license for the technology for our startup, which would include paying for the legal fees associated with the patent.

TOP THREE TAKEAWAYS:

1. If you discover something cool in a lab that you want to turn into a company, it is your job to file the patent through your university. This ensures you are protected and can talk about the technology to potential investors and partners and even publish papers about it. It also means you don't have to come up with the thousands of dollars needed to file a patent right away.

2. Even if you aren't sure you have something valuable on your hands, talk to your university's IP office before you publish anything or give any public talks about it. They have likely seen more of these deals than you and will be able to quickly determine if it is worth going through the patent process.

3. If you discover something new without using university resources, you are free to patent it on your own, which lets you avoid having to negotiate a license from your university down the line. However, you must then either foot the bill for a patent application yourself or risk telling people about your discovery without the protection of a patent. If your discovery is valuable enough, no one will give you money unless you can show you are able to protect it, and a patent is often the best way to do this.

#1 Lesson Learned: If you think you've discovered a cool new technology and can imagine a use for it, it's probably worth patenting, and you probably have an obligation to tell your university either way. You *have to* submit a patent application before you present your idea anywhere that *might be considered public*.

About Marco: Marco Lobba is the CEO and cofounder of Catena Biosciences, which is focused on developing transformative protein and cell-based therapies using their patented coupling technology. Marco received his PhD in 2020, from UC Berkeley, where he worked jointly between the labs of Professor Matt Francis and Professor Jennifer Doudna on protein modification approaches to CRISPR/Cas9 delivery.

MENTORS BY JAMIKA AND KRISTI

As a first-time startup founder, one of the most important things you do is spend time with somebody who has experience you lack. I found this mentorship to be particularly helpful when you're a student-founder with lots of questions. The right mentor can not only provide tips and feedback on your work, but can also make connections for you (think introductions to potential clients and partners, manufacturers, marketing or legal help, or generally provide recommendations for organizations, funds, programs, or partners who are good to work with). Getting the right group of mentors can give you a leg up on your startup journey. So how do you find them?

It's possible your university has an entrepreneurship center or program. That is the first great place to look and where our featured founder in this chapter found her mentors. It's also wise to look outside the university: Does your city have an angel investor group, incubator, accelerator, or other startup community you can plug into? These are other great sources of mentors. It also might be wise to approach your university's alumni association to see if there is an alumnus working in your field who might be willing to connect with you. Finally, you can leverage platforms like LinkedIn—you can search for individuals who attended your university and work in your field, and use the university as common ground to kick off a conversation.

Today, with everything being online, it's easier than ever to find mentors. And they're eager to find you! Here are a few tips to make the most of a mentorship experience:

1. Prepare your questions ahead of time and have a clear objective for the meeting.
2. Have a succinct elevator pitch or company overview ready.
3. Share any materials on your company (pitch deck, website, social media, etc.) with your mentor ahead of the meeting.
4. Be prompt and understand how valuable your mentor's time is.
5. Thank your mentor after the meeting.

If you'd like to read more on this topic, you can check out the Techstars Entrepreneur's toolkit module on engaging with mentors: https://toolkit.techstars.com/engage-with-mentors.

More on mentorship from Jamika.

FEATURED STORY:
Jamika Martin,
Founder, ROSEN
Skincare, UCLA, Business
Economics,
Graduated 2017

I've dealt with difficult skin most of my life, so from a young age, I was well aware of the solutions on the acne market. Fast forward to my sophomore year in college; I had recently finished my second round of Accutane, but I was back at square one when it came to my skin. At this point, I realized the solutions for breakouts (over the counter and cosmetic) hadn't changed in the ten or so years I had been using them, so I set out to create a solution.

ROSEN began with me searching for more desirable acne treatments and ingredients that were backed by modern studies. Once I found a few I was particularly interested in, like Tea Tree Oil or Zinc Oxide, I literally started mixing products together in my dorm room. I bought some small bowls, spatulas, and whisks and went into product development mode because that's all I could afford. After about a year of playing around with the idea, I had the opportunity to pursue it on a larger scale after I earned my undergraduate degree and participated in the Startup UCLA Summer Accelerator. From there, I was able to truly test and market the brand and take the idea from a small, hand-made skincare line to a brand that had the bones to grow.

The first time I dove into ROSEN full time, I was immersed in the Startup UCLA Summer Accelerator. If you've ever done an accelerator, you know how mentor-heavy they are. This was honestly the best thing for me because I'm typically fairly heads down in my work and try to figure out problems on my own; however, as a startup founder, you quickly learn that is no way to grow. Finding mentors who have helped define the direction of my brand has been like second nature to me, but it's not always the most straightforward path.

I have always found mentors through my connections. I think more often than not, people will email experts to try to get them to become a mentor. While this is totally doable, I encourage startup founders to build within their own network. I found probably 50-75 percent of my mentors through introductions from a previous mentor, and each has been just as helpful as the last.

TOP FOUR TAKEAWAYS:

1. Regularly update your current mentors so they always know what's going on and what you're struggling with.

2. Always be willing to hop on a call and get acquainted with another founder, expert, or partner. You never know who they may connect you with or what insight they may have.

3. Clearly ask questions. For example, if I have supply chain issues, I'll email everyone I know who has expertise in this area with a clear, succinct question that they can easily answer.

4. Thank your mentors. Be clear that you are grateful for their time, and show them how you put their advice into action! No one wants to keep giving out advice if it never gets used.

#1 Lesson Learned: Stay in touch with everyone. You'd be surprised who might be helpful and who might connect you to someone else.

About Jamika: Jamika Martin is the founder of ROSEN Skincare, a brand that's working to create the next generation of acne care. After years of dealing with difficult skin and a lackluster selection of skin care products, Jamika began formulating products while studying business economics at UCLA. Upon graduating in 2017, she pursued ROSEN full time in the Startup UCLA Summer Accelerator program. Since launching her company, Jamika has grown ROSEN Skincare from a small startup on a bootstrap budget to one with thousands of customers, securing partners such as Target, Urban Outfitters, and Nordstrom.

Next, we'll hear an expert opinion from Kristi. Kristi has worked with thousands of mentors through her work with Techstars. She knows the ins and outs of how to get the most out of a mentor relationship and shares her tips. Kristi rocks!

ALL ABOUT MENTORS
by Kristi Walthall,
Global Mentor Catalyst at Techstars

No matter where you are, it's important to surround yourself with brilliant people who can help guide you and your business forward. The journey of building a business is an ongoing learning process that involves learning about yourself, your team, your product, your customers, and your company, and turning experiences into relevant information to improve as you go.

Mentorship matters and can bring irreplaceable value to you and your business. In my mind, a great mentor is a person who has made all the mistakes possible in a narrow field. Then, by freely sharing their wisdom and guidance, they can keep you from acquiring some of the scars they have received along the way.

Mentors are often experienced entrepreneurs or subject matter experts with deep expertise in business, industry, or technology, who also have the right personality to help you navigate the challenges of high-growth entrepreneurship. They work with you pro bono, without expectation of reward or compensation, share their knowledge and counsel, and will open their networks to you when appropriate.

It's important first to identify the right mentors for the current state of your business and then to optimize your interactions with them to accelerate your success.

Identifying Your Mentors

There are many qualities that make for a good mentor—many of which are outlined in the Techstars Mentor Manifesto found on the Techstars website. Look for these traits in new mentors and cultivate them in your existing mentors. A good mentor should be:

- Self-aware and honest—mentors know what they don't know and say so.

- Empathic.

- Authentic.

- Direct.

- An excellent listener.

- Responsive.

- Able to separate opinion from fact.

- Committed.

- Trustworthy—mentors hold your information in confidence

- Someone you connect with on some level—a mentor who doesn't connect with either you or your business won't be motivated to help.

In addition, mentors should:

- Have domain expertise (the knowledge and understanding of a particular field) and deep experience.

- Use the Socratic method—mentors should not tell you what to do but rather ask you the right questions so you can think for yourself and make good business decisions.

- Provide specific and actionable advice.

- Challenge you to think about the problem in different ways.

- Make introductions where appropriate.

- Expect nothing in return—a great mentor isn't going to say, "Sure, I'll make that intro for you, but I want x percent of the sale."

- Dive deep—the mentor who will dive deep with a company, who gets down and dirty with the product, the business, the customers, and the financials, can be the most helpful.

Where can you find good mentors?

It's important to build a strong, proactive network now, so you can activate that network when you need it. Building a network with trusted relationships is vital to success. The closest relationships always yield the best results. You can build your network and find great mentors by:

1. Leveraging your existing network. Look for people with the traits mentioned above who are directly connected to you or connected with someone you know.

2. Identifying and building connections with entrepreneurs at local tech companies.

3. Scanning through the mentor lists of other early-stage startup programs, universities, etc. Mentors in these programs love mentoring, whether they are local or not. Reach out and share one to three sentences that describe your business and a specific problem you'd like to cover in a mentorship session if they'd be willing to connect with you.

4. Attending and building relationships with experts at industry meetups and events.

Remember, you can truly learn something from everyone you meet. It's important to be open to listening, learning, and growing as you interact with others and build your mentor network.

Getting the Most Out of Mentor Meetings

Now that you've identified and connected with the right mentors, it's important to understand how to engage them to get the most out of your time with them.

Productive mentor meetings are opportunities to address challenges and gain insights that could change the course of your company. It's important to:

1. Research the mentor prior to connecting and come prepared with questions.

2. Have a team member take notes so you can engage and listen intently.

3. Learn to redirect the mentor if they go down a rabbit hole that you don't want to explore.

4. Synthesize the mentor's takeaways at the end of the meeting and follow up with a personal thank you email or note.

5. Communicate how you implemented their feedback. Remember: you don't need to take a mentor's advice (it's your company); however, you can give feedback on how you *considered* a mentor's advice and went another way. It helps mentors learn and shows engagement on both sides.

6. Send the mentor updates as you make progress.

7. Continue to build the relationship with your mentor.

Surrounding yourself and building relationships with excellent mentors who are generous with their time can be game-changing for you and your business. Best of luck out there!

About Kristi: Kristi Walthall is passionate about building the community around startup founders to help them succeed. As Global Mentor Catalyst at Techstars, Kristi works to empower mentors to help other entrepreneurs succeed.

COFOUNDERS BY BARRY

In the early days of starting your company, it's important to find cofounders who not only balance your skills, but whom you can trust. It might sound cheesy, but I truly think of the cofounder relationship like a personal relationship. First, you go through a dating phase to see if you get along; then over time, you learn about each other, run into conflicts, and see how you work together to overcome obstacles. If things work out, you might decide to get married. Think about finding a cofounder like you think about dating. This is a serious relationship, and the person (or people) you work with in the early days of your company can make or break your company's success.

I was fortunate enough to get really lucky with my cofounders. My first cofounder was another electrical engineer I had worked with for years on other extracurricular projects on campus. Because we had already worked together for some time, we knew our strengths and weaknesses and how to move projects forward together. We were also good friends with a trusting relationship. The two of us were on the technical side, and we knew we needed a cofounder with business and finance expertise to balance out our engineer brains. We got incredibly lucky finding our third founder. One day, a JD-MBA (combined juris doctoral and master of business administration program) student contacted me saying he had read an article about what we were working on and was excited about the idea. He offered to help however he could. This was a great sign that he would be a great cofounder—he took initiative to reach out to us, he expressed passion for our idea, and when we met him, he wasn't talking about equity or joining the team in any formal sense—he just wanted to help. The three of us ended up being a dream team. I was best at business development and operations, my other engineer founder was the technical lead, and our third founder handled all aspects of finance.

The following story from Barry describes his experience finding cofounders and top tips for identifying the right people. Sure, you can certainly start your company on your own, but we all know we're not great at *everything*. Finding cofounders can make your startup experience much less lonely, and it also means you have double, triple, or maybe even quadruple the time to work on various aspects of your company.

FEATURED STORY:
Barry McCann,
Founder and CEO, NUA
Surgical, NUI Galway,
MSc, Research Master's
Degree in BioInnovation,
BioInnovate Ireland
College of Engineering,
Graduate 2018

I am not your average student-entrepreneur. Next month, I'll turn the big four-O. I'm married with two beautiful kids, a dog, a mortgage, car loans, etc. My academic background consists of a degree in business and a master's degree in medical device innovation, with seventeen years between enrollments. Back in 2000, when I entered the National University of Ireland, Galway, as a first-year undergraduate, I believed my coursework would provide me with the tools to be successful in business, whether it was my company or someone else's. My aim was to get experience before starting a company—I would need this for credibility. I genuinely never considered starting a venture while in college. It may sound like an excuse, but there wasn't the precedent for college startups or the support systems in place like there are now.

Sports have always played a big role in my life, and for a long time, I thought my entrepreneurial debut would be opening a sports shop, but I never had the balls to do anything about it. After almost fifteen years of various business development and fundraising management positions, I decided to apply for the BioInnovate Ireland Fellowship, a year-long, full-time master's program run out of the National University of Ireland, Galway. BioInnovate is an affiliated program of the Stanford Biodesign Fellowship where the objective is to identify unmet clinical needs and use the biodesign process to develop a commercially viable startup company. Although I was based in the same university, there was a stark contrast in student-entrepreneurial activity and supports. Think-tanks, launchpads, hackathons, and mentorship programs were all new additions from my previous experience but are now embedded in the student ecosystem.

From the moment I applied for a place in the BioInnovate Fellowship in 2017, I was committed to developing a startup. I had left full-time employment, which put my family under some financial strain and definite financial uncertainly. I already felt like an entrepreneur by taking such a risk. My clinical research area was obstetrics and gynecology, and for ten weeks, I shadowed doctors in theaters throughout the country to identify truly unmet problems within women's health. The following months were spent researching and brainstorming potential solutions. At the end of the fellowship, it was time to commercialize my idea. For this, I would need a team and funding, in that order. I don't know how many times I've heard that venture capitalists invest in the team as much as the product, so it was vital to get the right people to work with before taking on the world.

It is exciting to start a business, but don't let the adrenaline rush you into choosing a cofounder. It is not a task to be taken lightly. In 2016, entrepreneur Sujan Patel wrote a supportive article on Entrepreneur.com regarding the traits you should look for when selecting a cofounder. I only discovered the article after our founding team was established, but I can thankfully say that we tick all the right boxes. I consider the most important of Patel's criteria to be:

1. **Complementary strengths:** make sure they bring something new to the table, and for this to happen, you must recognize your own strengths and weaknesses.

2. **Hungry for knowledge:** a willingness to learn is required in any organization, and the concept of constant improvement should be a value held by all founders.

3. **Shared passion:** a cofounder who recognizes your drive, mission, and passion and shares it is vital for success but also hard to find.

4. **Integrity and honesty:** finding the right partner isn't just about skills—it's also about character. Demand 100 percent honesty at all times.

For my startup cofounder, I also required specific engineering skills and experience relating to medical devices. Overall, I spent about six months networking with not only those whom I deemed appropriate to be a potential cofounder, but with anyone who could introduce me to a potential cofounder. I cannot stress enough the importance of building your network early and constantly working on expanding it. Speculate and connect with people who, at some point, you might like to have a conversation with. When the time comes, your network will contain many of the important stakeholders who will open doors for you and your venture.

#1 Lesson Learned: Building my business has been an around-the-clock endeavor, so having a cofounder whom I trust, who has my back, and whom I get along with outside of work is vitally important. Do not settle for anything less.

About Barry: Barry McCann is the CEO of NUA Surgical, an award-winning startup innovating in women's health. Barry is a NUI Galway laureate with almost twenty years of commercial and fundraising management experience, most recently within the MedTech industry. In 2019, Barry was named Best Senior Entrepreneur at the EIT Health Alumni Needs-Led Innovation Showcase in Lisbon, Portugal. In 2021, he received the JCI Ireland Outstanding Young Persons Award for Medical Innovation. He lives in Galway, Ireland, with his wife Tory and two children, Teddy and Elsie.

HIRING BY MARIO

I f finding cofounders is one of the most critical actions you can take as a new founder, hiring people is certainly a close second. Even though your staff may not literally have ownership in your company, in many ways, they might own your ability to be successful.

With my startup, we found our best workers on campus. They were students who were excited about our technology and also had experience working in the areas we needed help with. For example, our first intern was another electrical engineering student who already had experience developing hardware and software for robotics projects and had his own consulting clients. We knew we could trust him to do stellar work because we had seen his work on the robotics teams. We knew he was excited to work with a startup because he was already dedicating nights and weekends to his side projects.

Finding on-campus talent is definitely a great place to start. If that fails, you can try asking around your network to see if friends, colleagues, or professors can suggest resources. If this fails, try connecting to your local startup community to see if members (other startup founders) can recommend talent. And if all else fails, there's always Fiverr.

The story that follows features Mario, a student-founder who realized he needed help when his company started to grow. Mario shares his experience with finding talent at this early stage.

FEATURED STORY:
Mario Micale,
Founder and Principal,
Narrative Digital Media,
The University of Akron,
Business Administration,
Graduated 2017

I had known for years I liked video. My career in video actually started in sixth grade when I made a video for an assignment instead of writing an essay (because I hated writing—ironic, isn't it?). It was terrible, but really got me accustomed to that medium. Years later, my passion for it really took off when I helped create a viral (for the time) video for my high school that ended up receiving a lot of attention and even got some coverage on the local news stations. I found out years later that this single video was responsible for completely filling two years' worth of class enrollment for the school. I love bringing to others the joy and excitement they feel when they see a video or piece of content that speaks to them. In college, I continued to do odd jobs here and there for companies and individuals, and I filmed weddings on the side outside of being a full-time student and being involved with numerous student organizations. I had very little free time. When it came time to graduate, so many of my friends had really cool jobs working at companies in marketing departments, sales, etc. After years of working several jobs and internships and experiencing a lot of environments, I decided to take the leap and build my video company into something great.

Starting out, I was the only person at the company. I wore all the hats, which I quickly realized wasn't sustainable. You only have so much time in the day, and at some point, you have to trust someone else to do the work. Trusting someone else to represent your company and what you've created is a huge hurdle to overcome, and it took me some time to come to terms with the idea. Once I did, I started working with some talented individuals here and there to help as needed, but then a huge project came along. A local university needed to significantly increase their video output. Their own internal video team just couldn't keep up with demand. They reached out, and after some negotiating, ended up hiring us! It was so exhilarating and thrilling since it was one of the largest deals we'd closed. However, soon after making the deal, reality set in. How would I have the time to keep up with this new partner? There was only one of me, and they needed a crew of three. Would I need to stop growing the business? I needed to find good people to work with and train, fast.

Who was my first call? My colleagues—the people I had met through networking and in school. Some of them had started their own businesses, and others I had developed relationships within lots of different environments. They were extremely helpful and ended up pointing me in the right direction to find talent. After some time, I ended up contacting former professors and the directors of on-campus programs. I explained my situation, and they put me in touch with really great students to consider for the project. I spoke with many passionate and skilled individuals, and after some time, ended up hiring the perfect person to help me do an incredible job for the client. The person was such an asset that they still work with me today—they are one of my most talented editors.

TOP THREE TAKEAWAYS:

1. You can't do everything yourself. You will need to hire others to grow your business. Trusting someone takes time, but documenting your processes and what is important to you goes a long way in guaranteeing quality.

2. Your local contacts and universities are amazing resources for finding talent. People in these institutions are extremely well connected to other people, not only in the university, but also the community.

3. You will be amazed by how much you can grow your network and build your team right at your local university—you just have to ask.

#1 Lesson Learned: Understanding your weaknesses as a startup founder or owner is critical to finding people to work with. Having self-awareness and honest conversations with yourself about what you're really good at and what you aren't will make it abundantly clear where you need the most help and when you should hire someone. Once you understand that and tap into your local resources for talent, you'll be able to build an incredible team of talented people around you and grow your company.

TEAM MANAGEMENT BY VARIKA

At some point in your startup journey, you'll have to think about hiring and managing a team. It's possible you might not have much team experience yourself, let alone team management experience. What I've learned is that you could read countless books on management and leadership, but what successful team management really comes down to is excellent communication. My favorite book on this topic is *Crucial Conversations* by Joseph Grenny, Kerry Patterson, and Ron McMillan.

So much of running a startup is about having great communication skills. With my company, I was fortunate to have great friendships with my cofounders and teammates. We worked together and hung out together, but it didn't stop there. We also had regular team meetings, had established communication systems, file storage systems, and organizational systems. You might think, *Oh, we're just a startup. What do we need all that for?* I can tell you that being organized and effectively managing communication and tasks within your team will pay off tenfold, especially when you start to work with partners, investors, or customers.

In this chapter, Varika's story includes a number of amazing tips for building and managing a team. She shares insights on where to find talent, how to structure a job description, and how to build a positive team environment. In parallel, you might find this Techstars Entrepreneur's Toolkit module on EQ (emotional intelligence for entrepreneurs) helpful: https://toolkit.techstars.com/eq-for-entrepreneurs.

FEATURED STORY:
Varika Pinnam,
Cofounder, IDA, The
University of Texas
at Dallas, Marketing,
Graduated May 2021

When I was a sophomore in college, I joined a campus accelerator program to learn more about entrepreneurship. I knew there was a pitch competition at the end of it, but I went in with no business idea and no knowledge of the startup world. I decided to pitch anyway just to improve and get better, if nothing else.

My sister and I were brainstorming one day when we both said at the same time that there should be something to help entrepreneurs. "And it should be about ideas but called IDA and that will stand for Ideate, Decide, Act!" I remember quickly following up. It felt like the words just came out of me on their own. We had both worked with female startup founders in the past and witnessed the issues they faced, and when we began looking further into it and discovered so many statistics about the struggles of female startup founders, we knew we were onto something. At that time, we had barely any knowledge of the market or competitive landscape. We relied on Google and put together a pitch with the idea for a platform that offered female startup founders a community and resources. We ended up placing third, prompting us to keep going. Since then, we've pivoted several times to better address the problem and differentiate ourselves, but our mission has stayed the same. We exist to empower entrepreneurs to Ideate. Decide. Act. on their business dreams.

About a year and a half after that first competition, we had the realization that to kickstart our growth and product development, we needed to invest time in creating a much bigger team. We went from a team of two to twenty-plus nearly overnight. Along this journey, I learned a lot of lessons about leadership and managing teams. At its most basic, leadership is execution and inspiration. But it's more than that. It's navigating roadblocks, delivering hard news, and acknowledging that you don't have all the answers.

When you understand your own ups and downs and the startup journey, extend that understanding to your team. So, if someone can't make a meeting, needs to take several weeks or a month off, has family conflicts, stress, exams, or anything else going on, lead with grace and accommodate their needs as best you can. At IDA, we've been able to accommodate all requests every time, and as a result, have had a really positive, enthusiastic, fun group of people who are excited to work on the startup. Place trust in people and they will return you the same kindness.

TOP THREE TAKEAWAYS:

Here are the three main things I did to set up for the team, manage them, and prepare for future growth:

1. We recruited our core team entirely from Indeed and sourced some additional members from Fiverr and Upwork. As with many other student-led, campus startups, we began with other student interns. Make sure to write a really compelling, robust job description describing the benefits of joining your team and the skills needed, and don't undercut yourself just because you are a student startup team. Candidates can still learn a lot and gain a positive experience by being part of a fluid, innovative startup environment with a friendly team, and that is an attractive prospect. Set clear requirements in the job description and for yourself so you can sort through all the applications easily. I struggled with this myself in the beginning.

2. We made it a point to schedule a team building night every two weeks, and it's been really helpful for the team to feel like they are actually coming together and getting to know each other by interacting outside of work. Some team-building activities we've done are: Among Us, Skribbl, Spyfall, Icebreaker, Two Truths and a Lie, etc. You can also do digital Jackbox games, happy hours, group activities/crafting after mailing out a package, virtual scavenger hunts or escape rooms, etc. if you have the access/budget. Encouraging open communication and checking in with the team at the beginning of every meeting and giving them space to share their lives, updates, and things like that goes a long way.

3. We have been fortunate to have a certified scrum master and agile coach helping out with our team meetings and structure. (An agile coach is someone who specializes in agile methodology of software development and leads teams to work together better and more efficiently). I've learned a lot from him. I want to highlight a couple of key takeaways about running product development and teams in an agile way:

a. **User stories:** Break up your project tasks into descriptions consisting of the user interaction and the benefit. Make them small enough to finish within one sprint (however you define it—ours are one week currently). User stories also need a definition of what "done" looks like and what you need to test to make sure it actually meets that criteria. Doing these and assigning them to team members inside GitHub (a popular version control software that developers use) has been really helpful for not only staying on track but helping the team to feel invested in creating a good outcome for our users.

b. **Demos:** In each meeting, everyone does a demo of what they have done and discusses where they are stuck, what they plan to do in the next sprint, and what they need clarification on. Going through these four components for every member, every standup meeting without fail has made our meetings so much more effective and leaves everyone feeling more confident about product development.

#1 Lesson Learned: The number one thing I learned from this experience is that communication is everything. Your success is based on the way you communicate your passion, which gets the team excited with you, to the way you communicate the requirements, which can vastly differ from what they understood, all the way to practicing kindness and patience in your communications, which makes a huge difference and your team will actually notice and appreciate the experience when you lead with empathy.

About Varika: Varika Pinnam co-founded IDA, a marketing tech platform for entrepreneurs and brands, with her sister, Ghanika Pinnam. She went to The University of Texas at Dallas where she majored in marketing and minored in computer science. She is interested in entrepreneurship, venture capital, and technology.

R.E.S.P.E.C.T. BY MARIO

I remember the feeling of standing up in front of a room full of people who were thirty-plus years my senior to pitch for some grant funding. I remember the dreaded feeling of getting to the end of my presentation and just waiting for them to ask me ridiculously hard questions derived from their years of experience. I could feel them judging me, a twenty-something female founder of a cleantech company. What did I know compared to them? On this day, however, I was pleasantly surprised. I was able to answer all their questions and maybe even teach them something. When I left the room, some people from the audience came up to talk to me and congratulated me on my pitch. All of a sudden, I didn't feel like they were looking down on me, but rather, treating me as an equal. This was the first step in realizing that if I know my product and my company inside out, and I speak with confidence, I can and will earn respect from those more experienced than myself.

As a young startup founder, I bet you may be encountering similar thoughts. You might have imposter syndrome, or simply shut down when you're faced with a situation where you're the youngest in the room. In this chapter, we'll listen to a story by my friend Mario about his journey to gaining respect from his clients as a student-founder.

As I said earlier, my video career started back in the sixth grade. In college, my video company was young and I was working hard to keep it going. Starting out was rough. I can't tell you how many times I had been in a room with someone who was twenty, thirty, or forty years my senior, and me being a twenty-one-year-old college student trying to persuade them to give me money was always a challenge, and I mean *always*. One thing I've learned is, if you can, first grow facial hair (it adds ten years, trust me). But mostly, know what you're talking about. Practice your speaking skills and really understand your stuff. People older than you are more likely to respect you if you demonstrate knowledge and skill. If nothing else, they'll sense ambition and may see you as a way to benefit themselves. Either way, convince them that you know what you're doing and can make them better because of it.

Mark was one of the people who really helped get my company off the ground. He needed a series of training videos for his company of sales consultants, and through networking with my university, had chosen me and my company to create twelve videos over the course of a year. I had experience making videos, but this was a completely new challenge. To keep a long story short, after several meetings and discussing what the videos would look like, we filmed and edited them. During an editing review session, we were discussing business and what we were looking to do in the future. He said something that still sticks with me: "Well, your business really can't grow or diversify."

That still resonates with me. It's not so much that I want to prove him wrong, but I always wanted to grow beyond a videographer. I wanted to be a respected solution for companies, a partner they could rely on and trust to make meaningful video experiences for them. That training video project was so crucial because it allowed me to have money to invest in better equipment and better marketing and to really start to grow my business. Ever since he uttered those words, I have been focused on how I can build my company and use my resources to grow a business, not just a service. This year (2021) he reached out to me for some consulting work. He needed help getting a livestream solution up and running so he could continue sales coaching remotely, since that is the world we are living in now. As the years passed, we offered live streaming solutions since my mindset was always to serve the customers' needs. I told him what we do for livestreaming, showed him a case study and example, and confidently explained exactly how the team and I set people up for live streaming success. It was very clear to him I knew what I was talking about, and we made an agreement to consult on a livestream setup.

TOP THREE TAKEAWAYS:

1. Understand what it is you do and be knowledgeable about it. It obviously will depend on what your business is, but people older than you know you don't have a lot of experience yet. Convince them that what you lack in experience, you make up for in knowledge and skill.

2. I've found that older people, heck most people in general, usually look out for their best interests. If you can prove you and your company will benefit them by providing a valuable product or service they can't get anywhere else, you'll have their attention.

3. Communicate and be confident in yourself. Actually go help people. I understand sometimes it can be scary and there's so much you don't know. That's okay! Work through it, deliver value, and never stop learning and improving yourself and your company.

#1 Lesson Learned: Keep learning and growing. Respect is earned. In my experience, you earn respect by not only excelling at something and being confident in your offering, but also by respecting others and being genuine in your intentions.

About Mario: Joseph Mario Micale graduated from UA in December 2017 with a degree in business marketing and a minor in media production. Immediately after graduation, he began full time at his video production company, Narrative Digital Media, LLC, which he launched as a student. Since making videos in the sixth grade, he has continued to improve his media and storytelling skills. He loves bringing people together through his talents and takes pride in creating compelling stories and engaging content for everyone.

STARTUP COMMUNITIES
BY ALYSSA AND IAN

Starting a company can be a lonely experience. I'd argue it's even lonelier when you're early in your career and all your friends are busy having fun, partying, playing sports, or whatever students are into these days. When I started my company in college, as far as I knew, I was the only student on campus who was trying to start a company. I felt lost at times, wishing I could find just one other student who was going through the same experience. A few years after starting my company, I was on the hunt for connections and attended a local angel investor meeting. During the announcements, a guy named Rick stood up to talk about a group called Launch League. Rick talked about hosting "founder dinners" where anybody working on a startup could gather to share ideas, help each other, and sometimes, just vent. I was eager to find out more about this startup community and started attending events. As soon as I plugged in, I felt stronger. I had peers to share my struggles with, new avenues to meet mentors, and more ties to local funding sources. The connection to this founder community not only changed the trajectory of my startup, but also my career, and arguably, my life. I found lifelong friends in that community (six years later, that guy Rick officiated my wedding) and connections who continue to support my career.

Even in today's world with virtual-everything, many aspects of your startup journey rely on local resources. Today, it might be easier to find connections to other founders on your campus or in your local community. In this chapter, we'll share some ideas on how you can find your community.

First, we'll hear from Alyssa, a startup founder who felt the strain of starting up alone and built a community to support herself and other founders.

FEATURED STORY:
Alyssa Petersel,
Founder and CEO,
MyWellbeing, New York
University, Master's in
Social Work,
Graduated 2017

Someone told me in the first ten weeks of starting MyWellbeing that starting a company is like a fifty-year career condensed into five years. I could not agree more.

For all the highs—the lives you change, the team you build and bond with, how much you learn—there are lows—the fundraising challenges, the hires who fall through, the beloved teammates who move on, the problems that feel impossible to solve.

What I realized quickly was that people who were not startup founders did not understand why I cared so much, or why I took the highs and lows of MyWellbeing so personally. It was as though MyWellbeing and I were one and the same.

While I do believe that part of our work as startup founders is to increasingly create more space between our personal identity and the success or failure of our company, there is a very real element of our personal identity within our company that drives its early success. This is a visceral experience that only other founders can truly understand, which can be lonely and confusing in isolation.

Connecting regularly with other founders offers invaluable support, especially for first-time founders, solo founders, and marginalized founders.

I was lucky to start MyWellbeing at NYU through the Summer Launchpad Program (SLP). SLP had been running for some time (and continues to), so there were multiple years of cohorts. As part of the program, the staff would bring back alumni of the program to speak on panels. During the year following my participation in SLP, the team at the Leslie eLab also put together a regular meeting of alumni and conversations with industry leaders in marketing, fundraising, sales, product, and more.

Over time, naturally, we (the alumni of SLP) bonded. We supported each other through highs, lows, and everything in between.

I started to notice that we would spend endless hours sound-boarding our business problems and needs, and sharing business tools and resources, while (intentionally or not) sidestepping our emotional highs, lows, and needs. I was craving a supportive environment to share the emotional highs and lows transparently, vulnerably, and with a group who would really get it.

I started something called Founderhood, which we continue to this day. We meet the first week of every month and talk about anything and everything on our minds, particularly, how we're feeling emotionally. We aren't necessarily seeking answers, although often, one or more of us has "been there" and we're able to share what helped us through. We are primarily seeking support, recognition, camaraderie, and connection. And that is exactly what we foster and share.

TOP THREE TAKEAWAYS:

1. As a startup founder, it is invaluable to identify, join, or create a safe space where you can connect with others who are likely to understand your experience and whom you do not need to "perform" in front of.

2. Being a founder will lead you to bond nearly immediately with other founders, and may lead to feeling misunderstood or lonely in other relationships. Setting expectations with yourself, your team, and others in your life whom you do not work with will support the health and longevity of your relationships inside and outside of work.

3. Beyond business resource sharing and troubleshooting, it is equally, if not more important to listen to and support each other emotionally. The founder experience is unique, and we are too often encouraged to be superheroes who do not have human vulnerabilities. When we address and embrace what makes us human with community support, we become stronger and more resilient leaders.

#1 Lesson Learned: Identify three to ten startup founders you relate to whom you can meet with regularly (once a month recommended) to informally share, process, and support each other. If you cannot find a pre-existing group that resonates with you, create one. You may not actively think you want or need this support, but getting into the practice of sharing regularly, processing, and supporting will bring you resources you didn't know you needed and will empower you to become a stronger and more resilient leader.

About Alyssa: Alyssa Petersel, LMSW, is founder and CEO of MyWellbeing (mywellbeing.com), where she and her team connect people with the *right* therapist, while supporting mental health providers in building their businesses and professional communities. Named Forbes 30 Under 30 2021, one of Crain's New York Business Notable Women in Healthcare 2019, and one of Built in NYC's 50 Startups to Watch in 2020, Alyssa and her team have worked with more than 35 million people through mental health support and content and have been featured in prominent publications like *Forbes, Allure, HuffPost, Cosmopolitan, Glamour,* and more. Alyssa, also a writer and therapist, released her award-winning book, *Somehow I Am Different,* in 2016. A native New Yorker, in her off-hours, Alyssa enjoys spending time with her friends and family, supporting social justice, and learning more about others' cultures and world views.

Now we'll hear from Ian. Ian literally wrote the book on startup communities. He coauthored *The Startup Community Way* with Brad Feld in 2020. This book helps readers take their startup communities to the next level, using the theory of complex systems. Ian also spent time leading the ecosystem development team at Techstars where he breathed life into a series of initiatives that help startup communities (and the founders within them) grow. I had the chance to learn from Ian when I joined the team in 2021. I knew a chapter on startup communities wouldn't be complete without his explanation of what these communities are and how you can leverage them in your startup journey.

STARTUP COMMUNITIES HELP ENTREPRENEURS SUCCEED
by Ian Hathaway,
VP, Capital, Techstars

For university students contemplating entrepreneurship as a part of their career journey, a number of key factors need to be considered, such as what market opportunity to exploit, how to get early funding, when to time the launch, and how to assemble a strong team, just to name a few. But don't overlook two equally, if not more, important ones: where to pursue an entrepreneurial venture, and consequently, who to surround yourself with while doing so.

That's where startup communities come in. Startup communities are the people, relationships, resources, and support mechanisms that coalesce around entrepreneurs to help them succeed. Venture-building in and around collaborative environments produces better outcomes, and that's what startup communities are all about. Here are five reasons:

1. **Access:** The critical resources that power innovation today, such as ideas, knowledge, talent, and capital, are not exchanged in a purely market context but rather through networks built on trust and reciprocity. Relationship building is essential for entrepreneurial success; a startup community provides the platform for such connections to take shape.

2. **Ideation:** Proximity to other innovative and ambitious people provides exposure to ideas and methods that spark learning

and creativity in our own minds. This produces a virtuous cycle of ideation and collaboration that produces the conditions where breakthrough ideas emerge.

3. **Inspiration:** Nothing inspires entrepreneurs to attempt the impossible more than witnessing other people doing the same, particularly when they have a shared experience (such as being from the same city or attending the same school). This is especially true for young entrepreneurs looking for mentorship or connection with people who have already experienced one or more entrepreneurial successes.

4. **Support:** Building a high-growth startup is hard—really hard. It can take a toll on the physical, mental, emotional, and financial wellbeing of the company founders. It can strain personal relationships and undermine self-confidence. Having people on the journey with you who can deeply empathize with the experience of being a startup founder is essential.

5. **Joy:** Being part of a startup community is fun! Who else would you rather build relationships with than people who are passionate about many of the same things you are?

Okay, so that's the theory of startup communities, but how does someone actually go about participating in a startup community? Here are four practical tips:

1. **Be experiential:** The first step is simply showing up. This goes beyond the obvious point that you can't benefit from a startup community without actively participating in it. Instead, it's a prod to be exploratory—unabashedly so. There are a lot of collaborative communities to plug into, whether they are virtual or physical. Find what works for you.

2. **Be helpful:** The value of startup communities is determined not by what people get out of them but by what they put into them. The fastest way to build credibility and respect in any community is to look for opportunities to add value and help others without asking for something in return. By giving first, you'll get more than you could ever imagine.

3. **Be committed:** Relationships are not formed overnight. Being a leader in your startup community requires consistent participation over a long period of time. By making a long-term commitment to the community—ideally a decade or more—the startup community can be seeded with lasting values that take shape around the entrepreneurs.

4. **Be a leader:** Mahatma Gandhi said to be the change you want to see in the world. If you don't have access to an active startup community, or if you do but it's not serving entrepreneurs in a productive way, band together with a group of fellow entrepreneurs and create one. Take action; don't wait. You only need a few like-minded individuals to get started.

Have fun! Let the work of building a startup community be an extension of what you love most: building great companies that solve big problems.

About Ian: Ian Hathaway is an investor, strategic advisor, entrepreneur, and writer. He is a leader on the Capital Team at Techstars, which is responsible for global investment strategy, capital formation, and fund management. Ian is also an active advisor and investor to early-stage startups and venture funds, and he is the coauthor of *The Startup Community Way* (2020) with Brad Feld.

NOT GOING BROKE
BY (ANOTHER) IAN

Finding money for your startup is hard enough, but how do you also support yourself financially? How do you pay for classes? How do you keep up with rent? I've seen a number of creative solutions used by student-founders, and each comes with its own advantages and disadvantages:

1. Live with your parents. I know, this doesn't sound fun. But I did this for three years of my college career and saved...get ready for it...more than $18,000 (and this was way back in 2008-ish when I was paying $500 a month in rent).

2. Work on your startup while you're co-oping or interning for a company that pays you a salary (maybe even your university entrepreneurship center). Because I studied engineering, I had to co-op every other semester. I was paid decently at this job, so that was a great opportunity for me to work full time and work on my startup nights and weekends.

3. Pick up a consulting gig. I had friends in college who picked up small consulting gigs to support themselves. You can work with your university to see if they have connections to potential clients. Whether you code, do social media, or have some other

skill, odds are a local company would be willing to hire you part time. (Note: This is also awesome for resume building.)

4.   Work for a startup.

5.   Go crazy with pitch competitions, grants, and maybe even asking your family for some extra money.

These are just a few ideas. You can get creative and combine them to come up with something entirely new. In the story that follows, Ian shares how he spent quite a bit of time being broke, but through a lot of persistence and something called an *opportunity list*, he found creative ways to support himself financially and build his startup.

FEATURED STORY:
Ian Howard,
Cofounder, Shower Stream, The University of Texas at Austin, Mechanical Engineering, Graduated 2017

During my last semester as a mechanical engineering student, I had the opportunity to choose a company to work with for a final engineering project. My options included engineer's dream companies like Schlumberger, 3M, Lockheed Martin, and other large, prestigious companies. And then there was a startup called Abstract Engineering, which was developing a shower alarm clock that enabled people to wake up to a warm shower first thing every morning. I couldn't find out anything about them online other than a one-page website and an outdated LinkedIn page, but my interest was captured. As you may have guessed, I went with the startup. I enjoyed the idea of my final engineering project making a real difference to the sponsor company, even if it didn't look as good on my resume. I became so invested in the startup and the vision that the project quickly took over my life, and I continued working on it after graduating, increasing the founding team from one to two members. Since then, we have refocused the idea to making a smart shower for hotels that saves water and proves the savings through data collected over Wi-Fi, and the rest is history.

While I was a student, and especially after graduating, I was completely broke. I was broke before starting my company, but afterwards, I not only had to make enough money for myself to survive, but I also had to fund the company. The costs at this stage are typically low, but for a hardware startup, they are much, much higher than software. I figured that I needed about $25,000 to develop a very early prototype and pay the founding team's rent until we could raise an initial funding round from investors.

Simply put, the solution was: The Opportunity List. This is what we called it. It was a running list of all the startup opportunities we could scrounge up from our network and online searches. It mainly consisted of pitch competitions, grant applications, startup show-cases, and networking events. The purpose was to: 1) win pitch competitions for cash prizes, 2) meet wealthy individuals known as "angel investors" who would write small checks, 3) get your startup talked about in the right circles. Oh, and another key strategy was begging relatives for money. Because if your family won't invest in your idea, why would strangers?

TOP THREE TAKEAWAYS:

1. Don't be scared of sharing your idea with everyone and their dog. Your idea is not special—your ability to execute it is—and no one is going to steal it.

2. A successful founder's number one quality is persistence. We lost countless opportunities before we had our first win, but that made the first win feel that much better.

3. It only gets harder. Your expenses will go up long before you are profitable, and raising millions of dollars is a lot harder than raising thousands.

#1 Lesson Learned: Persistence, persistence, persistence. It doesn't matter how smart, talented, or rich you are. Okay, it does matter how rich you are. But still, if you can push harder and last longer than your competition, you will win every time. Starting a novel company is a lot harder than you think it will be, and everything will take a lot longer than you think it will. The only way to win is to keep going. Good luck!

About Ian: Ian has a BS in mechanical engineering from the University of Texas. He has led technical engineering and entrepreneurial programs to install wind turbines in Tanzania and provide earthquake relief in Chile.

TIME MANAGEMENT BY JASON

One of your biggest challenges when starting a company in college is learning how to manage your time. From personal experience, I can tell you there is no magic formula to doing it all. Simply put, you *can't* do it all. You'll have to learn how to prioritize your time and decide where to put your energy. We all have the same hours in the day; it's what you do with those hours that matters.

I mentioned this earlier in the book, but during my college years, I decided to graduate a year later so I could slow down on my coursework and spend more time on my company. I also worked part time for a full year vs. full time (and still got credit for it, just half credit).

Jason, our featured founder for this chapter, gives lots of great tips on this topic, including the suggestion I mentioned above, taking fewer classes per quarter/semester. You definitely have options as a student—I highly recommend talking to an advisor at your university (and probably consult with your parents, too) to see what you can shift around in your schedule.

FEATURED STORY:
Jason Goodman,
CEO, Antithesis Foods,
Cornell, Food Science
(PhD), Graduating 2021

I co-founded Antithesis Foods while in my second year of working toward my doctorate in food science at Cornell. During a product development class, we were tasked with coming up with a healthy food of some sort, so we made a crunchy snack, kind of like a chocolate-covered pretzel, but we used chickpeas. This wound up being pretty nutritious and tasting great—we were still eating the leftovers after the class ended. I was always interested in entrepreneurship, so I started a company with some classmates to commercialize the idea. It turns out it is really difficult to start a business based on a brand-new food formulation, but with the help of the National Science Foundation, our team is now well on our way.

I started graduate school in Ithaca after working for five years in Philadelphia at Penn State. I had a great group of friends and family in Philly I could drive home to visit. I was also building friendships and a social life, getting into doctoral research, etc. in Ithaca.

If someone tells you it's possible to balance all of these things and start a company, don't trust them. If the startup is getting the attention it needs, you're going to have to prioritize ruthlessly. Here are the three steps to follow:

1. **Decide if you want to start a company.**

    At the core, make sure starting a company is something you really want to do. If you only want to get some entrepreneurial experience, join someone else's startup, or get an internship at one. If you want to run the thing, make peace with sacrificing weekends, vacations, getting As on tests, a really fun themed party you want to attend, the first day of good weather in the spring, etc. You can do these things; just accept that the startup usually comes first.

2. Maintain a kind of balance.

If the above scared you away, that's okay—starting a business is not for everyone. If it didn't scare you off, here's how I learned to maintain a kind of balance:

Schedule everything, and schedule startup tasks first. Block in what you need to get done to hit your company milestones; then fill in everything around that. Everything you want to do goes on your calendar app. Schedule blocks of free time, schedule blocks of class time, schedule "hang out with friends" time. You can even schedule a whole day off. By doing this, you won't feel bad doing the fun things you need to do to stay sane or taking time to study for classes or do research for your PhD. It works because you blocked time for the startup first; it has priority.

3. Decide what has priority.

You've decided that the startup is your number one priority; now decide which other projects you are okay with doing a "bad job" on. Will your friends remain your friends if you don't see them for ten days? Twenty? Figure that out because you cannot do this without their support. Are you okay doing a mediocre job in school? Maybe you need to do well in a specific set of classes—prioritize them. This is all about making a clear-eyed decision on which downsides you are okay with.I decided I would go very slowly on my PhD, so I would wind up graduating later than expected. I see friends from home once every couple of months, but this is generally scheduled far in advance, and I have canceled several times. I do attend a bunch of entrepreneur events. These are a great opportunity to socialize. The coronavirus pandemic was helpful in some ways because I could connect online with folks I would usually have to drive five hours to see. As the startup grows and you get more people on your team, you will get more time. However, in the early days, with a small team, you're going to be doing a lot.

TOP THREE TAKEAWAYS:

1. Make sure this is something you really want to do.

2. Ruthlessly prioritize tasks and be okay doing badly at some things.

3. Schedule everything.

#1 Lesson Learned: Starting and running this startup has been the most formative, educational, and worthwhile experience of my life. Though I've made a lot of sacrifices, I think they have been worth it.

About Jason: Jason completed his doctorate in food science, studying the intersection of taste, diet, and the microbiome at Cornell University. While at Cornell, he cofounded Antithesis Foods, a food technology company working to make better-for-you foods through cutting-edge food science. Their first product is Grabanzos, a crunchy chocolate snack powered by chickpeas. Prior to his work at Cornell, Jason worked in the pharmaceutical industry doing basic research on antibody drug development and neurological disease diagnostics. He holds a BS in microbiology from Penn State University and is a native of Philadelphia.

P.S. Jason recommends the following resource: "The Struggle" by Ben Horowitz https://a16z.com/2012/06/15/the-struggle/.

PART-TIME ENTREPRENEUR BY VAL

I f you're currently a student and also starting a company, you're going to find yourself working on both your company and your studies, at a minimum. On top of that, you might have a part-time job, a co-op, or an internship to work around. How do you manage it all? Will investors, partners, and customers look down on you because you're not fully committed?

I was never full time with my startup. I was either in college or working full or part-time while also working on my company. And that was okay for me. My company was in the early stages of developing our product and didn't have a defined market or customer prospects, so it would have been foolish for me to attempt to work on it full time. I believe fully committing to your company is important, but only when that is an intelligent decision for both you and your company.

How do you do it all? The following story from Val explains how he navigated being a part-time entrepreneur while continuing to build his company and find success.

FEATURED STORY:
Valtteri Salomaki,
CEO, EDGE Sound
Research, Inc., University
of California Riverside,
MBA with a Concentration
in Information Systems
and Marketing, Graduated
March 20, 2020

Building a startup is no easy task, and it's only harder when you are a graduate student or working a full-time job. Take it from me—I was crazy enough to work on two startup ventures while being a full-time MBA student with a double concentration on top of working part-time at a tech company called ESRI.

Sound exhausting? I won't lie to you. At certain moments, it was miserable.

Do I regret doing it? Absolutely not. It was actually the most rewarding two years of my life.

To pull off starting my own company while in school, I had to set a very strict schedule for myself and stay disciplined. Each morning I would wake up at 6:30 a.m. so I could get to work by 7:30 a.m. This allowed me to be done with work before noon, giving me enough time to eat and complete any unfinished assignments before heading to class. Three times a week, I would go to the gym after class to help destress and maintain focus. Every evening was dedicated to my startups; I set aside three hours, splitting the time equally between my consulting company, Free Logic, Inc., and my audio tech startup, EDGE Sound Research, Inc. One day a week, I did not work at all so I could recharge. Working every day will drain you and hinder your overall efficiency.

This schedule gave me a minimum of eighteen hours a week

to work on my startups, which was plenty to ensure they continued to gain momentum. I set specific milestones for myself based on validating each startup's growth and that they were worth going "all-in" on upon graduation.

After graduating, it is important to have a plan for how you will keep your startup moving forward. This either requires a part-time job or budgeting and finding cash for one year's expenses in advance to allow you to focus on your startup full-time. The most important thing is to maximize available time and reduce safety nets (such as a full-time job) that may mentally hold you back from giving your startup all you've got.

This is precisely what I did. After completing my MBA, I calculated exactly how much cash I needed to focus on my startups for a year without worrying about finances. I eliminated any extraneous expenses and moved back into my mom's apartment. In May 2020, during the pandemic, I left my job at ESRI and dedicated myself to my startups full-time.

TOP THREE TAKEAWAYS:

1. Create a strict schedule and stick to it. Time management is key to building a venture while being a graduate student or full-time employee because, otherwise, excuses will hold you back from giving your startup a fair chance.

2. Schedule personal time in your day and take one day off per week. It is important to focus on your mental health and identifying what outlets help you refresh after long days of work.

3. Create a means to get capital for yourself before going all-in, and reduce any safety nets holding you back from focusing on your startup.

#1 Lesson Learned: Pace yourself as you build your venture alongside your other obligations. It is more important to be consistent and spend a little time each day on your startup than attempting to work ninety-plus hours every week and burning yourself out. Building a company is a marathon, not a sprint, and it's the stamina to keep pushing an idea forward that will lead to eventual success.

About Val: Val co-founded both of his entrepreneurial ventures as a student while leveraging his tech career. He aspires to grow the entrepreneurial ecosystem in the Inland Empire (Southern California) and support other entrepreneurs on their journeys.

A̶G̶E̶I̶S̶M̶ ̶A̶N̶D̶ ̶S̶E̶X̶I̶S̶M̶ BY KATE

A while ago, I joined a clubhouse conversation with student-entrepreneurs from across the world. I was taking questions from these students, and over the course of an hour and a half, the number one question I got was related to age or lack of experience and how to navigate that barrier in the startup world. The second most popular question was about women founders and how to deal with sexism and a generally male-dominated investment world. The underlying answer (from both myself and the audience) came down to one simple concept: *confidence*.

The story I told you earlier about my experience pitching in front of a room full of investors who were years my senior speaks to this. As cheesy as it might sound, if you believe in yourself and enter a room with unshakeable confidence in your business, your plan, your value proposition, etc., the environment around you will respect you.

The following story from Kate, whom we first met in Section One under "Degrees and GPAs," describes her experience starting a company with her sister at a young age in a male-dominated field. Their ability to rise above these challenges shines through in this story.

FEATURED STORY:
Kate Madden,
Cofounder and
Head of Global
Sales, FenuHealth,
University College
Cork, Food Marketing
and Entrepreneurship,
Graduating May 2022

Entering any industry at the age of thirteen and fourteen would be challenging because it is difficult to get people to take you seriously at that age. Also, for my sister and me, entering the equine feed and supplements industry was going to be a huge challenge because it is primarily male-dominated. I never believed in male domination, and I could never understand how that concept could even exist until I entered the equine world and realized it was mostly men. When I was growing up, the idea of horse riding seemed very female-dominated and was portrayed as a feminine activity; therefore, I expected the business world to be the same—but our mentors told us it was not. My first experience of male dominance was when we took our first trip to Equitana, the equine trade fair in Germany. Over the course of the weekend, we did not meet one female business owner or leader, which, even though I was forewarned, I still could not properly comprehend. Yes, our mentors had warned us that this was going to be the case, so we were somewhat prepared to handle these situations, but the reality was disheartening. Being two young Irish sisters who were blossoming entrepreneurs trying to find a place in the male-dominated equine world became a lot more daunting after our trip. But we did not take this negatively. We decided to turn our disadvantages into our advantages, and that is how we began and continued to thrive and grow within a male-dominated industry.

Once we accepted that we would be surrounded by men, we needed to figure out how to get them to treat us like business-women and not two teenaged students. The first thing we did was create a business uniform to begin building our brand. The uniform was simple. It was white jeans with a navy polo neck T-shirt and a navy sleeveless jacket, all having our label stitched onto the front. This was the first step in moving away from the schoolgirl image, because in Ireland, each secondary school wears a school uniform that differentiates their students from other schools. Our new uni-forms made us recognized for our business brand, not our school. After this, the greatest piece of advice we received was to be con-fident and own the room. It can be very belittling having older men and women make you feel small in a business meeting; we learned, instead, how to be the center of attention and control the meeting. This allowed us to gain what we wanted from meetings rather than being told irrelevant information from older businesspeople. Once we learned how to deal with not being taken seriously, we began to be a lot more productive in business meetings. Once you are confident and go in with a set plan and a list of goals, it makes the whole business meeting scenario more approachable.

TOP THREE TAKEAWAYS:

1. We learned how to deal with belittling and how to gain what we wanted from uncomfortable and awkward situations. It can be nerve-wracking entering a meeting room with ten middle-aged men sitting at one end of the table facing you and your younger sister and asking you difficult ques-tions. The first piece of advice and takeaway I got from this experience was to go into every situation with confidence. If you believe you know what you are doing and what you want, the people you are meeting with will also believe you.

Confidence is key, especially when you are nervous about a particular meeting—it is all about using your nerves to achieve!

2. Second, our motto in FenuHealth is "Never give up." This primarily comes from the fact that in the beginning, it was our 152nd formula that worked, and we always say, "What would have happened if we had stopped at 151?" Also, it is important to know that nothing good comes from giving up.

3. Finally, the last piece of advice I have picked up from experience is to "Keep It Stupidly Simple." I have learned that half of the time, the most experienced businesspeople do not understand their own industry's jargon. If you keep it simple, you will get more from a meeting and ensure others will understand what you want.

#1 Lesson Learned: Age and gender do not define you or your business. Your actions, values, and confidence do.

About Kate: Kate is a third-year student at University College Cork, Ireland. At the age of fourteen, she cofounded a business called FenuHealth with her younger sister Annie. FenuHealth supplies a range of products to the equine industry, particularly products related to stomach problems in horses. They now have nine people on their team and sell to fifteen countries worldwide.

TREAT YOURSELF
BY ALYSSA AND BEN

I think it's fitting to close out this section by talking about one of the most important aspects of starting a company, especially in college—taking care of yourself. It's so easy to get swept up in the excitement (and stress) of starting a company and lose sight of your number one asset: yourself. We've already talked about time management and learning to prioritize, but in this final section, we'll listen to two stories. The first is from a student who found a path forward through journaling, introspection, and finding the right support group to move his company forward. The second is from a student who experienced burnout and found ways to cope with her situation.

FEATURED STORY:
Ben Omarina,
Cofounder and CEO,
Lazarus, Texas A&M
University, Chemical
Engineering,
Graduated December 2020

In July of 2016, an ambush killed five police officers in the town where I live, Dallas, Texas. As a new citizen of the United States born in the United Kingdom, I often questioned the level of lethality in the nation I now live in and will start a family in someday. The idea that the United States has limited itself to choosing between excessive or ineffective force in a life-threatening situation concerned me. Law enforcement officers and citizens alike were limited to either ammunition built for destruction or incompetent weaponry made to stop individuals. The situation begged the question: Why do we not have a spectrum of lethality? Why isn't there an option that accounts for the preservation of life? Why don't we create ammunition that is built to save people pre-engagement? That is when I set out to become informed on the technology that could fill this gap in the market of lethal options and eventually patent a technology known as biocompatible ammunition.

I quickly realized that setting out to address a controversial problem in a life-or-death industry put my mental fortitude and ability to persevere to the test. I struggled to communicate a vision of preserving life when the lives being taken posed a threat to others. The journey to developing a company as a student was filled with constant doubt. A student-entrepreneur's life was largely unknown to me and not conducive to agile innovation.

One day I took a walk to a local park to reflect. I reflected on my experience as a student-entrepreneur and recognized the strength, discipline, and grit formed as a result of balancing a chemical engineering degree and starting an ambitious company that is on a mission to save lives. The reality was I could not have made progress without the people who were committed to the vision, nor could I have indeed run the race of a student-entrepreneur if I did not have people who were committed to me as a person. If I did not pause simply to acknowledge my gratitude for my network, I would have never been able to wake up every day with a purpose. The truth is that serving a vision and a company as a student is a draining, painful, and intense journey that is not for the faint-hearted. Nonetheless, for the brave souls committed to this journey, here are some takeaways.

TOP THREE TAKEAWAYS:

1. Build a like-minded community, a tribe of individuals who have bought into your vision and to enable you or anyone to make an idea a reality. During my time in college, I was able to sacrifice activities not connected to creating a company because the community I built had the same goal. In addition, my community also had a desire to connect and celebrate the small wins, improving my mental health by laughing and sometimes tearing up with people who understood.

2. Be faith-driven. Without some sort of source of truth or principle guiding your belief, you will never be able to create consistent action that leads to sustainable or monumental change for yourself or even for your company.

3. Make time for reflection. Journaling and documenting my intentions and outcomes became a grounding experience that facilitated clarity of thought. It is important to reestablish a new level of confidence daily because only then can you lead a group of individuals who have bought into the vision you create.

#1 Lesson Learned: If I could give one piece of advice to a student-founder, it would be to build a clear vision through journaling and to seek opportunities to serve a team of people who have bought into the vision and committed to your success.

About Ben: Ben is a December 2020 Texas A&M graduate and an experienced student cofounder and CEO of Lazarus Solutions, LLC, with a demonstrated history of working in defense technology.

This is such an important topic, I decided to include two stories. (Yes, this is a thing I've been doing, I know.) Here's another perspective from Alyssa, whom you heard from previously in the Startup Communities sub-section.

FEATURED STORY:
Alyssa Petersel,
Founder and CEO,
MyWellbeing, New York
University, Master's in
Social Work,
graduated 2017

Anxiety is no stranger to me. Born a colicky child, raised to be an A-plus student, and rewarded for high performance inside and outside of work, until recently, my self-esteem and internalized perception of "success" was fueled by external affirmation and accolades.

All of that said, it wasn't until I was training to become a therapist that I prioritized my own therapist search. I was what some in the biz call the "worried well"—my mental health was not interfering with my day-to-day functioning; I nurtured a subtle constant buzz of anxiety that I managed to brush under the rug for years on end, until I could justify a therapist search because it was a requirement of my professional pursuits.

I searched. And being the A-plus student I was, I searched hard, and I searched with finding the "perfect" therapist in mind.

I learned the hard way that finding a therapist is hard. I called dozens of providers without anyone calling me back. I asked my insurance panel for recommendations—I waited on hold; they provided a list of five names at a time, none of whom answered. I called again. And again. I booked consultation call after consultation call, failing to find a strong fit. I was frustrated, discouraged, and angry. All while searching proactively, meaning I wasn't in the depths of an episode of anxiety or depression, which would have made the search that much harder. I was training in the field, so I understood the acronyms, jargon, and alphabet soup woven into every head-shot-biography combo. Still, I ran into barriers.

After months, I found a provider who felt like a good enough fit, but I still wasn't sure. Simultaneously, I'd use platforms like Netflix to watch TV and movies—which provided personalized viewing recommendations for me—and Seamless to order takeout—which provided personalized food recommendations for me—so I wondered why personalization was not part of the mental health provider search.

As I started working one-on-one with therapy clients, I found the same problem existed on the provider side. Clients would come to me having chosen to work with me by my headshot alone, wanting to work through issues I did not have specific training in. After forty-five minutes of deep bonding and vulnerability, my clinical responsibility was to refer them to someone else. Essentially telling them, "Thank you for sharing your deepest, darkest, but I don't love you; try again." (These are not the words I used, but psychologically, that is how it can feel on the receiving end.) Sometimes, that rejection is enough to keep people out of therapy altogether.

I knew on a deep, visceral level through first-hand experiences on both sides, something needed to change. A fast, easy, personalized way for people to find the right provider for them would help tremendously.

I was nearly finished with my master's in social work at NYU, and I was familiar with a summer program where you'd apply with your business idea and, if accepted, receive $10,000 in non-dilutive funding (essentially a grant) to start and launch it. Perfect.

I, as a social worker with technically no business experience, teamed up with a colleague (also a social worker) and wrote up our business case and mocked up some early wireframes with Balsamiq. For those new to the startup and product world: wireframes are designs that you would generally hand to a technology developer to turn into a web or mobile application, and Balsamiq is a platform (give it a shot!) that makes it easy for non-technical visionaries to create those designs and translate the imagery they have in their heads onto a digital screen that others can see and understand. Long story short, we applied, demonstrating grit and resourcefulness as two hungry and passionate social workers, and we got in—learning later that we were the first social workers to be accepted and the staff was largely unsure whether we'd make it, but they were willing to take the chance.

Teaser: So much has changed in the four-plus years since that day, and yes, their taking a chance on us worked out.

A startup founder's biggest strength can also be their biggest vulnerability: We are insatiably passionate about what we're building.

While this relentless conviction and passion is what drives our business forward and is something to nurture, we need boundaries to separate our personal and professional time, and we need to fill our lives with more than work to sustain a long, exponentially growing, healthy life and career.

In my first three years building MyWellbeing, I experienced at least three periods of burnout—the kind of burnout that really knocks you off your feet, interferes with your day-to-day, and forces you to change.

Just before closing our seed round, I was restless. I wasn't sleeping well, I'd entirely lost my appetite, and I'd introduced friction into my personal relationships because of the hours I was working and how obsessed I was with my self-imposed work responsibilities, hours, and demands.

Once I reprioritized my focus and time, I made significantly meaningful strides forward in my personal and professional lives.

"Self-care" has been commercialized in the health and wellness industry, but taking care of ourselves is not a luxury. It is not fluff or a nice-to-have. It's an absolute necessity—both for our personal wellbeing and the health and growth of our business.

Sometimes, we need to slow down to speed up.

When I was forced to face the fact that the hours I was working and responsibilities I was owning were too much, I fiercely reprioritized where I was investing my time and energy.

I cut projects that were not absolutely necessary to move the most important needles at MyWellbeing. I reinvested time into therapy and coaching to better understand what internal narratives were driving me down a recurring path to burnout. I unpacked what I was going through with my founder community to learn about others' experiences, feel less alone and less like a failure, identify best practices, and get support. I started saying no, recognizing that every no is a yes to something else.

In many ways, an unexpected silver lining of COVID-19 was being forced to say no to regular evening programming that I thought I *should* be present for to extend our reach and network. Almost overnight, I had three to four hours per night back that I could reinvest in high-level strategy.

We began to work smarter, not harder. Though we went from working through the weekend to having at least one or two weekend days entirely off, the business thrived. We met and surpassed goals we previously struggled to reach. We secured more investment capital. We grew our team. Each step of the way, I prioritized exercise, therapy, and coaching to maintain perspective, learn lessons every day, and recommit each morning to what mattered most inside and outside of work.

Nearly one year after making some of these meaningful changes, our business is performing the best it's ever been, and I am happier than I've ever been. I do not feel shame or guilt when I receive and do not answer a Slack message after 11 p.m. I have a clear sense of what our focus areas are, and I confidently say no to opportunities outside of those areas, or more realistically, "Not right now." I have leveled up the caliber of talent joining our team and hear regularly from my team that my example and leadership style are two of the many reasons they take joy in working and growing together.

TOP THREE TAKEAWAYS:

1. Taking care of yourself is as important for your business as it is for you as a person.

2. Founders are under extreme pressure to "do it all" and "do it now." The more conviction you can generate and sustain about what your non-negotiable core focus areas are, the better you will be at driving those core KPIs forward and saying no to the rest, which are costing you time and energy.

3. Therapy and coaching are incredibly valuable assets. If you are not motivated to invest in either for your own sake, prioritize them as business investments that will drive your startup forward.

#1 Lesson Learned: Sometimes, it can feel like mental health is a luxury—something we'll get to later when we have more money or time. If we just answer one more email, pitch one more pitch competition, talk to one more investor...we'll get to mental health on the other side.

I cannot stress this enough: The state of your mental health will influence literally every other thing you do. The healthier you are, physically and mentally, the more successful you will be and the more success you will attract around you. Do not skimp on your mental health.

If you delay or postpone proactive mental healthcare for too long, the consequences of burnout will cost you more money and time than a regular, proactive investment in taking care of yourself. If you are not motivated to do it for yourself, do it for your business.

About Alyssa: Alyssa Petersel, LMSW is Founder and CEO of MyWellbeing (mywellbeing.com), where she and her team connect people with the *right* therapist, while supporting mental health providers in building their business and professional community. Named Forbes 30 Under 30 2021, one of Crain's New York Business Notable Women in Healthcare 2019, and one of Built in NYC's 50 Startups to Watch in 2020, Alyssa and her team have supported more than 28 million people through mental health support and content and have been featured in prominent publications like *Forbes*, *Allure*, *HuffPost*, *Cosmopolitan*, *Glamour*, and more. Alyssa, also a writer and therapist, released her award-winning book, Somehow I Am Different, in 2016. A native New Yorker, in her off-hours, Alyssa enjoys spending time with her friends and family, supporting social justice, and learning more about others' cultures and world views.

HOW CAN MY UNIVERSITY HELP ME START A COMPANY IN COLLEGE?

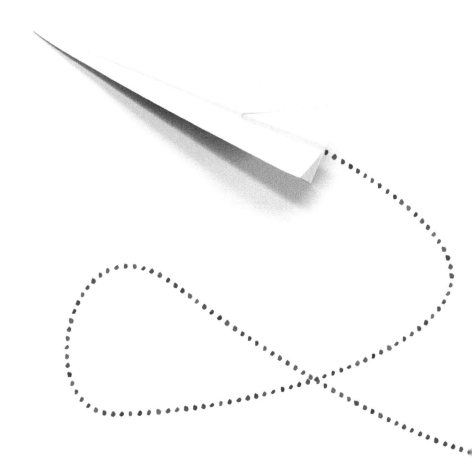

"If you cannot see where you are going,

ask someone who has been there before."

— J. Loren Norris

This section covers a big topic. Like, really big. Getting help from your university is one of the main reasons starting a company in college is a great idea. Your university probably has at least a few of the resources you will read about here. Here's the thing—they don't necessarily give you a roadmap to all this stuff when you go through orientation. My university, for example, didn't have a ton of resources. I found that we had an entrepreneurship institute that offered a few classes. But some universities have it all: accelerators, incubators, bootcamps, startup weekends, mentorships, pitch competitions, and so much more. If you don't know about these resources now, you can start to ask your professors, advisors, and classmates—they'll be able to point you in the right direction.

This section will walk you through all the awesome things your university has to offer. The students who contributed to this section will help you understand the benefits of the various programs and how you can use them. To top it off, we start this section with an overview of university entrepreneurship resources from Deanna at UCLA. Deanna is a director of entrepreneurship programming on campus and knows all the ins and outs. Soak it all in, go forth, and make the most of what your university offers!

UNIVERSITY RESOURCES BY CHARLOTTE, DEANNA, AND MIR

Being a student-entrepreneur has many advantages. Perhaps one of the best is the opportunity to participate in a plethora of classes, programs, and competitions your campus likely offers. In this section, we'll take advice from an expert on university entrepreneurship programs. I had the pleasure of meeting Deanna through my work with the LaunchPad network. Deanna is the LaunchPad director at UCLA, and she runs a variety of entrepreneurship programs on campus. In this chapter, Deanna gives an overview of those programs. Following this, we'll hear from students who have taken part in campus entrepreneurship programs and see how those programs changed and enhanced their journey.

EXPERT TIPS ON LEVERAGING UNIVERSITY RESOURCES
by Deanna Evans,
Director, Blackstone
LaunchPad at UCLA

Do you have ideas you can't shake no matter what? They keep popping up when you have everyday problems that really frustrate you, your friends, or your family. You start imagining solutions and improving systems for these problems. But you don't know what to do with your ideas or even what the first step should be. You are fortunate that today many universities have multiple entrepreneurial resources available, whether you are curious about starting your own business, joining an existing business, developing an entrepreneurial mindset and skills to increase your marketability when you graduate, or even getting help accelerating the development of a business you already created.

To begin, you need to understand what is happening in your university's entrepreneurial ecosystem on-campus and off-campus within the greater community. Here are areas to explore for undergraduate and graduate students:

Curricular programs can be directly related to your major or minor such as business and social entrepreneurship majors and entrepreneurship minors. These majors/minors will provide a more formal education and pathway to being an entrepreneur.

Co-curricular programs include incubators, accelerators, maker spaces, social impact initiatives, and more. These programs are a great way to supplement your non-business related major.

Why would you commit your time to these co-curricular programs when they don't provide college credit? *It's about learning by doing.* You will build knowledge, skills, and social and professional networks by participating in co-curricular programs. These co-curricular programs may provide an opportunity to receive mentorship, attend workshops and events, receive coaching, access legal office hours, use a dedicated co-working space, apply for seed funding, work within teams, create a side hustle to make money while going to school, and possibly get your first internship with a startup. For example, at UCLA, students can access the Blackstone LaunchPad year-round to meet with a venture consultant about their idea and get feedback on how to execute their idea. Or they can apply to Startup, UCLA's summer accelerator program, for an intensive ten-week bootcamp to gain traction for their prototype.

Student groups in the university entrepreneurship ecosystem have grown tremendously in the past ten years. Entrepreneurially-minded students are developing incubators, accelerators, events, competitions, workshops, hackathons related to startup creation, design, social entrepreneurship, and more. Student groups usually meet once a week and create activities for members and for the campus community. Getting involved in a student group is a great way to get to know other entrepreneurially-minded students, expand your network, and possibly build your own startup team. For example, Bruin Entrepreneurs and Sigma Eta Pi have led the way with developing innovative, student-driven entrepreneurship activities at UCLA.

Competitions are a great way to get seed funding, mentor attention and feedback, and raise awareness for your startup. Look for competitions at your university associated with curricular, co-curricular, and student group activities. For example, at UCLA, the Barry and Meredith Eggers Entrepreneurial Seed Funding Prize awards $5,000 annually to the winning team along with a mentor meeting with Barry Eggers, partner at Lightspeed Venture Partners. Also, look outside of your university for regional and global competitions that may offer larger amounts of funding. The Global Student Entrepreneurs Award (GSEA) by the Entrepreneurs' Organization is a global competition for students who own a business while attending college.

Entrepreneur network opportunities include the Blackstone LaunchPad, which is at forty-six universities and provides resources to student-entrepreneurs, including a summer LaunchPad fellowship and a speaker series during the academic year. If your university is part of a larger system, additional opportunities may be available. For example, the University of California system has programs and opportunities for entrepreneurs affiliated with that system. Check out regional and global entrepreneur resources available to you. There are always new resources being developed to support underrepresented student-entrepreneurs.

As executive director of Startup UCLA, I'm often the first person to hear a student's idea. I'm not going to tell a student the idea is good or bad, but I will guide them in thinking about the idea and the next steps in executing it. I recommend students start out with research, develop experiments, and be informed by the data as they determine their next steps. Given our virtual world, online resources are a necessity, and I highly recommend the Techstars Toolkit in those first meetings to provide a framework for creating your startup.

If you explore your university entrepreneurial ecosystem and find that you don't want to be an entrepreneur or work for a startup, then you can take what you learned and be an *intrapreneur*—use your entrepreneurial mindset to solve problems within a corporation. The most important part of your entrepreneurial journey is to learn by doing and use what you learn to inform your future career choices.

Enjoy discovering and navigating your university entrepreneurial ecosystem!

About Deanna: As Startup UCLA's executive director, Deanna leads the Blackstone LaunchPad, summer accelerator, faculty innovation fellows, and a social entrepreneurship summer institute for high school students. She consults with students early on about their ideas and helps them explore the next steps in executing the idea and identifying available resources and opportunities to meet their current needs. Deanna has consulted with hundreds of startups since LaunchPad began in 2014.

Now that you have an idea of the different types of programs you can take advantage of, the stories that follow will detail the students' perspective of participating in these programs. The featured student-founders describe how these programs helped them, and they share tips on how you can best leverage entrepreneurship programming.

FEATURED STORY:
Mir Hwang,
Founder and CEO,
GigFinesse, New York
University, Chemistry
and Psychology,
Graduated 2019

I've been on stage, playing drums since I was fourteen. Neither of my Korean parents were quite comfortable with me pursuing music as a career, so conservatories and music schools were out of the question. However, I was able to strike a deal: I'd take a more traditional academic path, but only in a city in which I could play. That is how I ended up at NYU, taking chemistry by day and playing shows across the city by night. It wasn't enough just to play the drums; to get reliable gigs in New York City, I had to be a concert promoter, a booking agent, and a manager all rolled into one. This experience was a crash course in just how rough getting bookings can be for independent artists. Everything about how we consume music has been touched by technology and innovation except for music in its purest form. GigFinesse wasn't born in a single moment of clarity; it was an idea forged by endless nights stressing over unopened email and un-played demo tapes. Finally, I told my cousin Ryan my idea for a tech-platform that could help fix what's broken in live music. Ryan decided to take the plunge with me, quitting his job at Google to come out and build GigFinesse with me full time.

GigFinesse is my and my cofounder Ryan's first company. Neither of us were business majors, so neither of us really had a background in the nitty-gritty, day-to-day things you need to do to build and run a successful business. There's an endless supply of books, podcasts, blogs, all available with the click of a button. The sheer scale of online resources can be overwhelming—I wanted to be able to cut through it all and build a network in real life made up of people in the same boat as I was, in the same high-pressure situations pursuing similarly imaginative and crazy goals. Being a first-time startup founder as a student is a singular situation; starting this company meant that my first job out of college would be CEO. This makes it hard to relate to the high-level executives and established engineers who quit their jobs to start their companies. Finding other student-founders like myself, juggling investors and profit and loss statements, while at the same time trying to knock out finals was so critical to me.

Then I discovered NYU's exhaustive resources for young entrepreneurs, including the Summer LaunchPad, $300k Entrepreneurs Challenge, InnoVention Competition, Startup Sprint, and many more. Rather than our student status being a weakness, the staff at NYU's Entrepreneurial Institute helped us turn it into a strength. As students, we were able to take advantage of non-dilutive funding opportunities, which allowed us to scale the company without giving up any equity, and which proved critical in building our fledgling business. Our status as students actually meant that we could get into more rooms and sit down with more people than we had ever thought possible. Not only did the knowledge and know-how of the staff come to inspire and inform our earliest decisions at GigFinesse, but the network effect connected us with some amazing mentors like Nobu Nakaguchi, cofounder and CDO (chief data officer) of ZOLA, and Kristina Chodorow, engineering partner at Google Ventures, who have been unbelievably gracious with their time and will continue to be an important part of what I'm building moving forward.

TOP THREE TAKEAWAYS

1. Don't hesitate to ask questions or ask for help. Relationship management is key; be respectful and thankful for everyone's time since time truly is money in a startup setting.

2. Customer discovery does not end. Be prepared to pivot and then pivot again.

3. Recognize that work/life balance is next to impossible, but try to grab little moments here and there to catch your breath.

#1 Lesson Learned: I swear by the 33 percent rule and highly recommend it to other first-time startup founders. One third of your network should be people you can learn from, founders who have stood where you stand, faced the challenges you're facing, and reached the other side. The next third should be people in the same boat as you—other young and hungry entrepreneurs whose energy, drive, and resourcefulness should inspire you. Your final third should be made up of people whom you can mentor, allowing you to give back to the same communities that nurtured you.

About Mir: Mir Hwang is the founder and CEO of GigFinesse, a music tech platform that is reinventing the way artists and venues connect. Mir and his team started out with do-it-yourself shows on New York City rooftops and have grown to managing music venues across the United States. Mir's dream is to leverage technology to democratize the live music industry.

Finally, we have a story from Charlotte. Charlotte has a unique perspective as both a student-founder and a program manager for student-entrepreneurship programs. Her unique experience positions her to give some great advice on what to watch out for as you participate in these programs.

FEATURED STORY:
Charlotte Sullivan,
Social Entrepreneurship Program Associate, Middlebury College, and Cofounder of May West

May West was a collaborative, milkweed-based textile line produced between 2015 and 2020. A native North American plant, milkweed has a symbiotic relationship with the monarch butterfly, an iconic pollinator species sadly on the decline. As a fiber, milkweed is warmer than wool, naturally water repellent, and buoyant. Establishing a commercial application for milkweed was a great opportunity to proliferate the plant and help sustain the monarch butterfly. May West designed garments using milkweed floss as a textile and insulation.

In addition to my work on this project, I was working full time at Middlebury College managing their undergraduate social entrepreneurship fellowship program. The program offers grant funding ($7,000 to be used before graduation) to a small cohort of sophomores, juniors, and seniors. What I have observed in the students who participate in this program is, for those who have a lot of prior commitments (including leisure time and social life), it actually can be quite difficult to use all this funding within three years.

I think the students who make the most of the program are those who are willing to pare down their other activities, thereby prioritizing the fellowship and accomplishing their entrepreneurial goals. One way they can do this is working creatively and diligently to receive credit for their entrepreneurial work outside the classroom by designing and completing independent studies, getting jobs as research assistants related to their projects, and creating their own major/minor (if the school allows this).

TOP THREE TAKEAWAYS:

1. Ensure you understand the difference between grants and stipends, and identify which the program is offering. For example, it may seem great to get a $10,000 check, but when you look at the time you'll actually spend on your project, it might not actually provide a living wage. If you can find programs that pay you an hourly rate, they might be a more viable option to ensure your time and resource needs are met.

2. Have a plan and learn how to handle your tax situation. For example, many of the students I work with are international, so funds they receive typically have a higher tax rate (if their work is being completed in the United States) than those who are residents. It is really important to know the true amount of the award you will ultimately receive based on various criteria regarding citizenship, etc.

3. Don't be afraid to ask for more funding if you need it. The worst thing that might happen is you are told no and you wasted some time filling out forms. Many colleges have more funds to offer, even if they don't expressly communicate their availability. Plus, this gives you practice building an abundance mentality!

#1 Lesson Learned: Respect reflection time. Make sure you give yourself time to actually feel and hopefully enjoy what you are working on. If you honestly aren't, don't be afraid to speak up to your mentors and supporters to say you either need help getting back on track or the work just isn't for you. It's important to live your truth and not do work out of obligation.

About Charlotte: Charlotte Sullivan helps facilitate the social entrepreneurship program at Middlebury College in Vermont. Charlotte was part of the LaunchPad network and participated in the LaunchPad Lift Cohort—a mentorship-driven program for ten student-led ventures. While Charlotte is no longer working with May West, she is still actively involved in supporting student-entrepreneurs.

ACCELERATORS
BY LAURA AND SABA

Countless types of student-entrepreneurship programs exist: startup weekends, bootcamps, hackathons, pitch competitions, fellowships, accelerators, incubators...the list goes on. What to expect from these programs, when and how to use them, and how to get the most out of them are questions you will likely ask. In this chapter, we'll focus on accelerator programs, specifically, how to approach your application and how to leverage these programs.

I know you'll learn a lot from Saba. Saba manages the Techstars Accelerator Pipeline. That means he oversees the process of selecting the companies that get into our programs. He knows what to look for in a pitch, he knows what to look for in a founder, and he knows what an accelerator can do for your company.

P.S. If you want to learn more about Techstars accelerators and the application process, check out our accelerator hub: https://www.techstars.com/accelerator-hub.

**ALL ABOUT
ACCELERATORS
by Saba Karim,**
Global Startup Pipeline
Manager, Techstars

Accelerator applications are the new business plan—at least in my world. In fact, I can't remember the last business plan I read, let alone wrote, but I have reviewed thousands of accelerator applications, which I think do an incredible job at helping to tell the story and status of your company.

The first thing to keep in mind is that the goal is just to progress to the next stage. Whether it's a discovery call or a more formal investor interview, you should say all you need to say to get them interested or curious enough to want to learn more. That should help you realize you aren't meant to try to do everything in one shot.

Also worth noting is that if you're willing to take investment dollars from any accelerator, you're not doing your homework. You've got to find a fit with their approach and thesis and genuinely like and know the actual partners you're going to be working with.

The four big talking points in building your startup are your solution, traction, problem, and people. We pursue them in that order, but their importance is reversed. Meaning: Focus on you and your team, share why you care about the problem so deeply, and show the progress you've made.

1. **Know your audience.**

    On the web page or form, it should say who will be review-ing your application. Use that information to inform how tech-nical you can be. For example, sometimes at Techstars, non-in-vestors take a first look at applications, so if you're using a lot of implied language or complex jargon, then you have failed to stand out during the first screen. Maybe even follow them on social media and get a feel for what they care about.

2. **Clear and concise.**

    Just like your pitch, the answer in the accelerator applica-tion should be brief but comprehensive. Note, I am not sug-gesting answers should be short; that would have the opposite effect—don't use big words when simple ones will work, be brief and to the point throughout, and avoid acronyms altogether. Just imagine you're talking to someone for whom English is a second or third language or like you're explaining to someone under twelve. Keep it simple.

3. **Completeness is key.**

    Sometimes multiple questions are hidden within sections; you don't want to miss those. Even if something is optional, fill it out where applicable because it's sometimes a test to see how far out of your comfort zone you are willing to go.

    For example, a video doesn't need to be big budget—just open your webcam app on your computer and record it. Hon-estly, this is an opportunity to show your personality, so don't just read off a script and repeat what's in other parts of the ap-plication. Show them who you are and what makes you unique.

    Showing a product demo can be as simple as recording your screen as you navigate your website, your mockups, or photos of your product. There's a ton of freelance marketplaces where you can get product demos made affordably.

Additionally, complete the profile section if one exists. You know reviewers will want to learn more about you, so make it easier for them by filling out your profile, adding a photo, your social media links, and so on.

4. Be vulnerable and authentic

It will be tempting to answer everything and speak as if you know it all and have figured it all out, but that is usually a bad sign. Investors, especially at accelerators, want to see which areas you need help with so they can start playing the match-making role with mentors in the network. The way Techstars talks about it is, we want founders who are confident, yet coachable, so show what you don't know.

Pro-tip:

Use some of the following terms to show your groundedness:

- "What we've found so far is...."

- "We're currently running an experiment...."

- "Our hypothesis is...."

- "In my experience...."

5. Clarity in writing

- Write the application in third person: "We're building this app for single people. There are 5 million single people living in X who we'll help with Y" instead of "We help you get into a relationship. We understand finding a partner is hard." You see how different that is? This is an investor pitch, not a product pitch.

- Notice the difference between "We are doing" and "We will try to." Every word matters and helps investors to understand the story and status of the company.

6.   Get someone to review it

If you're not sure how the application comes across, get a friend or mentor to review it. If you're really confident about your answers and want to submit your application, get two friends or mentors to review it. The point is, take your time and get an outside perspective either way. It won't hurt.

Hang in there! It can take fifty nos to get one yes, then one yes to change fifty minds. Of the companies accepted into Techstars, 30 percent had applied at least once before.

About Saba: Saba is the head of the startup accelerator pipeline at Techstars, based in Colorado. Prior to joining Techstars, Saba was on the founding team of several startups across Australia and the United States, one of which was acquired by Hubspot and others are either still active or have failed. Saba is an educator at heart and loves coaching and mentoring early-stage startup founders.

Our next story is from Laura. Laura participated in NYU's Summer LaunchPad, a nine-week accelerator program at her university. Here, Laura shares her experience in this program and other top tips for student-founders.

FEATURED STORY:
Laura Rocha,
Cofounder and CEO,
Dathic Inc, NYU, Master's
in Public Administration,
Graduated 2020

My career started as a lawyer in Colombia with a deep passion for helping local communities grow. In 2017, I arrived at NYU to pursue a master's in public administration, and while volunteering for organizations and corporations in the US, I realized that the Latinx population here had growing purchasing power and was becoming increasingly important to the economy, culture, and politics. However, information about this segment of the population was vague and misleading. Data for Latinx populations is generic, and usually all are grouped into one homogenous culture using outdated stereotypes; that makes it difficult for companies and organizations to understand the economic power of the Latinx community and the importance of diversity within that community. Together with my cofounder, Jose Daniel Ramirez, who holds a master's in data science from Columbia University, we decided to create a solution for this problem, and Dathic, our artificial intelligence (AI) startup, came to life. At Dathic, we work to create actionable insights about Latinx individuals and communities in the United States. In 2020, we incorporated Dathic, a data platform helping brands and retailers understand the culturally diverse consumer and using AI models to optimize their distribution and marketing, which helps brands connect with their desired audience.

Our goal was to bring to the forefront the actual power and diversity of the Latinx community with their own individual cultures, idioms, traditions, and foods, and also make data very actionable so it can really make a difference. We started doing analysis for companies and organizations voluntarily while in school, and we proved our data helped brands connect to Latinx communities. Later, we started doing consulting; we felt more passionate and motivated to solve the problem and see how we could help the community feel heard and understood by retailers, but we lacked experience in entrepreneurship and the US market. That motivated us to look for help and take part in an accelerator program.

For the NYU Summer Launchpad Program (SLP), which is an immersive, nine-week accelerator for startups led by NYU students and researchers, our main goal was to define a business model to fit our solution and lay the foundation for the company's growth. My cofounder and I had strong technical skills, but we were looking for business guidance, and the SLP program was exactly what we needed.

The SLP is a fast-paced, results-oriented, and highly-personalized accelerator program. It proved to be the best start-up bootcamp for us. Through weekly pitches to mentors, investors, and peers, we learned how to redesign, validate, and continuously test our solution by focusing on the customer's pain-points. The training we got from SLP gave us the business skills and confidence needed to pursue Dathic as a viable venture.

TOP TAKEAWAY

Our biggest takeaway during our time at SLP was how the program helped grow our vision from a consulting business to a software as a service (SaaS) company. We also met great mentors who later became our first investors. This was a huge win for us and a great aspect of being part of an accelerator program. We also established our legal company name and structure, one of the benefits the program offered, which gave us the foundation necessary to continue building.

#1 Lesson Learned: As a foreign student leading a Latin-female-founded venture, being able to build relationships with coaches, mentors, and investors has been a great advantage for us, so my advice to fellow student-entrepreneurs would be to share their ideas, ask for advice, and implement this knowledge continuously.

About Laura: Laura has worked as a consultant helping Consumer Packaged Goods (CPG) brands introduce products to US Hispanic consumers and applying technology and open data to optimize government benefits. Laura worked for more than nine years in government agencies and leading public-private infrastructure projects in her native Colombia.

ENTREPRENEURSHIP CLASSES
BY KYLEIGH

Sometimes it's difficult to know if you're getting good content online. You can follow tons of blogs and social media accounts that talk about entrepreneurship, but what if you wanted to learn it all in one place, at one time, without having to search and vet each source? That's where an entrepreneurship class could be incredibly helpful. This is especially true if you're attending a college or university that doesn't have a strong entrepreneurship center.

At my university, we didn't have any accelerator programs or incubators as discussed earlier. But we did have classes: Entrepreneurship 101 and 102—I took both. They were high-level introductions, but I learned everything from how to identify the best business model to the basics of how to pitch your product. In my class, I got to use my own startup as my class project and worked on my pitch with help from the instructor. It was a great way to get college credit (I used the classes for my business minor) and also get some extra motivation to work on my own company.

The downside to classes? Well, first, they cost money. Second, they may take more time or not be aligned with your schedule. I still think my decision to take a class was a good one. Even with the cost, the credit I received and the structured work-time I had to focus on my company was a win. In Kyleigh's story, we hear how her decision to tap into her campus entrepreneurship center and take classes helped propel her startup forward. She says without those classes, her company wouldn't exist at all.

FEATURED STORY:
Kyleigh Russ,
Cofounder and COO,
Govern for America,
NYU, MPA,
Graduated 2020

When I was getting ready to graduate from college, I wanted to work in education policy at the state or local level. However, when I began to look, I realized neither I nor the people in my network actually knew how to find the jobs I was qualified for. I went on to teach for several years. In that time, I saw the effects of funneling our nation's motivated, smart young people away from the public sector and not emphasizing creating a diverse public workforce. Despite best intentions, policy and programmatic decisions are passed down to communities without consulting anyone in the community. This often meant the programs and policies designed to help the community I was teaching in were actually harmful. Fast forward several years. I reconnected with my now cofounder Octavia Abell, who was working in state government at the time. We discussed this government pipeline issue and decided to do something about it. Several months later, Govern for America (GFA) was born.

A month after we first talked about the concept of Govern for America, Octavia and I started to think about what it would actually take to get this idea up and running. We didn't know where to start. We had a long, written document that Octavia had been working on that described what we wanted to do and what the model could look like. She had talked to some people about the idea, but to actually follow through on this idea was a different challenge entirely. We didn't know where to start, how to incorporate as a company, how to talk to customers, or how to get in front of the right people.

I started looking around campus and discovered NYU had a university-wide entrepreneurial institute at the Leslie eLab. After a conversation with one of the coaches, I decided the Institute could be an amazing resource for us, and we applied to two of their programs—the Summer Spring and the Summer Launchpad. While we waited for a decision, we attended several of their classes, and I started using GFA as a case study in my regular classes at NYU. I can confidently say that without the coaches at the Entrepreneurial Institute, GFA would not exist today. They coached us through tricky decisions, connected us with experts in the field, and gave us space to make hard decisions. At the end of our summer with them, we launched our official first recruiting season and have since found incredible success. Three years later, we have placed forty-two people in government positions, designed an incredible curriculum, hired a team of six, and are heading into our fourth recruiting season!

TOP THREE TAKEAWAYS:

1. Ask thoughtful questions early and often. I have been amazed by how generous people are with their time when guiding young entrepreneurs.

2. If someone says no to you the first time, figure out why and ask again once you have addressed their concerns. Sometimes a small, simple fix can be the difference between a yes and a no.

3. Try to use your company or idea as a case study in your classes as much as possible. I used Govern for America as the lens through which I took all my classes, which meant I was both taking my classes and working on GFA at the same time. It's a win-win.

#1 Lesson Learned: Ask good questions and be truly open to the answers. Don't act on everyone's advice, but you should listen and consider what the experts are telling you and then make your own decision.

About Kyleigh: Kyleigh Russ is Cofounder and COO of Govern for America. Govern for America imagines a world where our most dynamic young leaders see government as an avenue for meaningful change, and our government reflects the values and diversity of our nation.

Section Four

I STARTED A COMPANY IN COLLEGE, WHAT NOW?

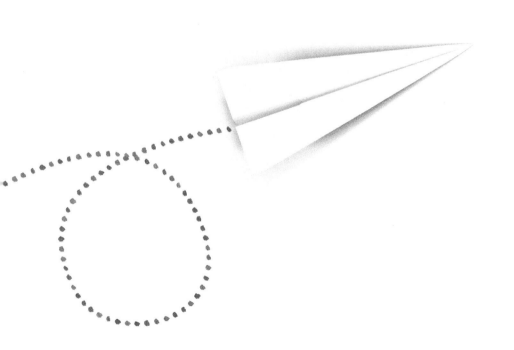

"The question isn't who is going to let me;

it's who is going to stop me."

— Ayn Rand

INTRODUCTION
by Scott Issen,
Co-Founder and CEO,
Future Founders

So you jumped off the metaphorical entrepreneurial cliff? Congratulations! Most people don't have the courage to take a chance on themselves—or an idea they are passionate about. It's worth celebrating this milestone and recognizing that you are special... and about to take the ride of your life on this rollercoaster we call entrepreneurship.

I work with young founders every day, so I know the decision to get started is also the beginning of many other challenges. Do I have what it takes to be a founder? Can I generate a sale? What if I don't find product/market fit and have to pivot or shut down my business? It's easy to dwell on these questions, but don't let the fear of what's ahead paralyze you.

My advice: Start small and stay focused. Create and work toward some short-term milestones that will help you demonstrate traction and allow you to celebrate success. You are building a business, so sales should *always* remain your focus. I know you may like creating social media content or entering pitch competitions, but you need to grow your sales if you want a successful business.

Surround yourself with other founders who are in your same stage of business development. You will need to lean on each other constantly and have people who believe in you and remind you that you are not alone in this journey.

Trust your instincts because you are the founder and it's your company to lead. You will need to learn how to filter other people's opinions and focus on doing what's best for you and your business. Just because other founders are raising capital or focusing on their exit strategy does not mean those are the right strategies for you... at least right now.

Worst-case scenario, you can return to school, pivot, or even shut down your business. Those are not bad things at all. It takes most founders multiple tries at entrepreneurship to succeed. And the network you've built and the experiences you've had as a founder will make you more marketable to other startups or employers should you decide to get a job. So don't worry—by pursuing your startup, you are already developing your "Plan B."

This section is all about just that: what happens after you start your company. We talk about whether or not students should consider dropping out of college, what to do if their startup doesn't work out, and how to leverage their experience to enhance their career overall.

Good luck as you embark on this journey, and remember what we tell our entrepreneurs at Future Founders: DO SOMETHING. **BOLD.**

About Scott: Scott Issen is Co-Founder & CEO of Future Founders, an organization that seeds diverse founders into the entrepreneurial ecosystem and has served 35,000+ youth in Chicago and across the country. Previously, Scott was Managing Director at the Chicagoland Entrepreneurial Center, which now runs 1871, and mentored high-growth entrepreneurs. Scott is a member of Entrepreneurs' Organization (EO) and The Economic Club of Chicago, and he recently finished his board term at Mishkan Chicago. He graduated magna cum laude from Washington University in St. Louis and was named to Crain's "40 Under 40" list.

DROPPING OUT BY MATT

You've started a company and things are really starting to take off. You start to wonder: Will I have enough bandwidth to continue my education while also managing my company? Do I even need a college degree?

You're probably familiar with many famous entrepreneurs who dropped out of college—Steve Jobs, Bill Gates, Richard Branson, Mark Zuckerberg, to name a few. But then there are others, like Elon Musk, Sara Blakely, and Jeff Bezos who earned their degrees (or even multiple degrees). How do you know if dropping out is right for you? The answer is: It depends. It depends on many factors, including the stage of your company, how much runway (money left in the bank) you have, what your sales pipeline looks like, and overall, how likely you are to recover and find other employment if you drop out, your company fails, and you're left searching for your next move.

You know from my story that I decided to stay in college. My company had many years of technology development ahead of us, so in many ways, it was better to stay in college and continue to work with the resources we had there.

But perhaps you're more fortunate than I was, and your company is really taking off. Here, we'll listen to Matt's story as he shares his reason for his decision to drop out of Syracuse University.

When I got to college in 2018, I started a medical virtual reality hardware company called Visos. It quickly gained traction, and in the year and a half after founding, we had made significant progress and formed partnerships with some of the largest companies in tech. However, in early 2020, COVID hit, and we soon found the market was no longer able to support healthcare-specific VR solutions like Visos. At the time, I had been very interested in language technology, and I had built an in-house product to help Miles (the cofounder) and I write email faster, using artificial intelligence. After the market shift, we decided to go all-in and focus on the email product. Since then, we've been building OthersideAI, which allows users to write a simple summary of what they want to say, and our AI turns that into a full, well-written email message.

As an entrepreneur working full-time on my company, I found it very difficult to also complete my classes and participate in typical college activities. I soon found I had to make a choice—stay in school and put the business on the back burner, or drop out and focus completely on the business.

I tried to work with university administration to work out a way for me to stay in school while running my startup. However, we weren't able to come up with any feasible long-term solutions. Due to the time I was spending on my startup, I wasn't doing very well in my classes, and I realized I wasn't on track to graduate in four years.

On top of that, running a startup doesn't require a degree, and the investors I met didn't seem to care that I wasn't a college grad. I decided to drop out to run my company full-time. One year later, my startup had raised capital from Tier-1 VCs, and we're growing incredibly quickly—dropping out of college was the best decision I could have made.

TOP THREE TAKEAWAYS:

1. If your startup is growing, and you need to decide between staying in school and running your company, it's okay to choose your company—you can always go back to school, but the startup opportunity you're chasing might not always be there.

2. School isn't the only way to learn. In fact, many people find that they learn much more by running a startup since you will need to learn finance, marketing, sales, technical topics, public speaking, and more on the job, depending on the industry you're operating in.

3. If you're set on building a company backed by venture capital investors, it is nearly impossible to do so while in school. A bootstrapped, or self-funded business is doable, though.

#1 Lesson Learned: Think about why you're starting a company—if it's just a fun hobby, stay in school. But if you know it is what you want to do with your life, college might not be worth it, so think deeply about whether it makes sense to stay in school. Yes, it may be scary to take the leap, but if you're set on building a large company, it's the best decision you can make.

About Matt: Matt is the cofounder and CEO of OthersideAI, which creates cutting-edge AI-powered communications tools. Previously, Matt founded Visos, a startup developing next-generation virtual reality software designed for medical use, and FURI, a company aiming to democratize access to sporting goods by creating high-performance products and selling them for fair prices.

NETWORK BY SAM

Perhaps the most valuable part of your college entrepreneurial experience is the people you get to meet along the way. When I worked with my startup, I met the owner of a new engineering consulting firm. Years later, after I had left my startup and was looking for a new job, that owner remembered me. He reached out to me on LinkedIn and was wondering if I was looking for work. I ended up taking a full-time job with that company. That is just one small example of how incredibly important your network is.

By *networking*, I don't just mean exchanging business cards. To have a truly valuable network, you must invest in *relationships*. When you meet someone whose experiences you value, stay in touch with them. Send check-in emails or grab a coffee once a quarter. Every job I've had since my startup has come through someone in my personal network, but that's because I stayed in touch, offered to help when I could, and genuinely cared about their wellbeing. I found they always returned the favor.

In this chapter, we'll hear a story about leveraging your network from one of our student-founders, Sam, who found a way to build a vibrant network by working with his university.

FEATURED STORY:
Sam Hollander,
CEO/Cofounder of FSCL,
Syracuse University,
Advertising and Finance
(Dual Degrees),
Graduated 2021

As a student strapped for cash as I described above (Section Two), I realized that to build a category-defining product, I'd need to know the right people. However, I didn't have many connections in finance—I didn't know where to start. To build connections, I looked for resources available to me at my university. I went to countless professors who had experience in finance, I spoke to the executive director of the launchpad at my campus, I spoke with other student-founders, and so many others. Every person I spoke with was either able to: 1) provide me incredibly useful insight into the industry, or 2) connect me with someone who could provide that insight. Entrepreneurship isn't necessarily about being lucky or having a lot of connections—it's about maximizing your resources and opportunities to create connections.

TOP THREE TAKEAWAYS:

1. Your network is your net worth. Seriously, when people in high school told me this, I'd go crazy, trying to figure out what they meant. It was hard to realize this until I put it into practice. Maximize your network. Tell people about what you're doing and what you're working on—they're usually more than happy to help. Networking and keeping in touch with your network is one of those invaluable things.

2. I've learned that beyond building your network, it's just as important to stay engaged and connected to the people in your network. Every few months invite them for coffee (albeit virtual), or schedule fifteen minutes to catch up. It's not a one-way street—just like you want to keep in touch with your network, they want to keep in touch with you.

3. Don't be afraid to ask for help. When I was first starting out with my company, I was afraid and embarrassed to ask people in my network for help, advice, and expertise. You should never be afraid to ask for help from your network. You never know what background or experience someone might have, and furthermore, whom they may know in their network.

#1 Lesson Learned: If I could give one piece of advice to a student-founder looking to grow their network, I would say it's very important to talk with as many people as possible. There are times when I'll ask different subject matter experts the same question, and more often than not, they all have different answers. In the real world, you're going to have to balance those different viewpoints and perspectives to form something that makes sense for you and your business.

About Sam: Sam Hollander is a Syracuse University senior studying finance, and advertising, with an emphasis in financial and investor communications, graduating in December 2021. He is also the founder and CEO of FSCL, a company pioneering the use of alternative finance vehicles to build a more simple, affordable, and flexible solution to financing higher education. @samhollander

PLAN B BY ANONYMOUS

What if your startup doesn't pan out? Whoa. That's a big question. But you know the odds of a startup becoming the next Facebook. It's a great idea to figure out what happens if it doesn't happen. My startup didn't work out. But, hey, I found an amazing career as a result of my startup experience. I would have never imagined how happy I could be in a career. It's okay if it doesn't work out.

How do you figure out a backup plan? What do you do if your startup doesn't pan out? First, let me say the world is your oyster if you spend any time in a startup…if you know how to leverage it properly. You've acquired amazing team leadership and communication skills, countless technical skills, and the list goes on. This is exactly what employers are looking for today.

Fear not. Even if you don't become the next Steve Jobs, you will find that this experience has been *amazing* for your job prospects. Our anonymous contributor describes their experience in the story below. Enjoy.

FEATURED STORY: Anonymous

Our company originated during the summer of 2017 when my cofounder realized there were a lot of sacrifices being made by corporations and businesses when traveling between cities that were close enough to drive to, yet more than an hour away. This meant that people would sacrifice valuable time either behind the wheel or waiting in TSA lines and checking into flights. We realized there was gap, and that if we could sell to a couple of hundred regular commuters between Dallas, Houston, and Austin, we could really tap into something huge. We went on to create a door-to-door, city-to-city transportation service that used Teslas to increase EV (electric vehicle) adoption and make travel easier for the consumer. We built something we hoped frequent travelers would really love. We eventually grew our business to accommodate clientele like Shell and Deloitte, and bring in over $155,000 in annual revenue from my junior to senior year of college.

Around the time COVID-19 became a worldwide pandemic, we saw our demand drop sharply. And in a matter of weeks, our revenue dropped to zero. More notably, for myself, I was in a super-awkward position. I would be graduating in May 2020, so I had to figure out what I would do next—assuming travel would stay the same for at least another year or so.

The team and I had to figure out what we could do next. Would we pivot to a different customer base? Use the cars for deliveries? We spent some time during the pandemic working with a couple of local initiatives like Good Apple, delivering produce to those in need in the Austin area, and delivering tacos and other goods to frontline hospital workers in the Houston area. But it just wasn't enough for me personally, and I felt like it was time for me to move on.

I leveraged my startup experience when looking for a position—something few people can look to (especially at the ripe old age of twenty-two). I'm not saying you should build a startup so you can pad your resume. I'm saying it's a great experience to look back on when trying to stand out from the field.

After leaving the company over the summer, I began to think about the different industries I wanted to work in—creating a list of companies I wanted to work for and how I would best approach them. Coming from an entrepreneurship background, I was lucky to have a plethora of mentors and colleagues who were able to give me advice, introductions, and even referrals to different positions and companies during my job search. I couldn't have done it without some of the professionals I met through the startup community, both on campus and off (Techstars especially).

Just because you're looking for another career or interviewing for a job doesn't mean you stop wearing your entrepreneurship cap. It just means you have to start thinking about entrepreneurship in a different way. Maybe it looks like a side hustle, like a newsletter, a podcast, or a community. Maybe it looks like working full time at a small startup to get the same experience of building one from scratch. Whatever it is, just because you're not the CEO or cofounder doesn't mean you're not an entrepreneur. Build on your own time and schedule.

TOP THREE TAKEAWAYS

1. Failure is awesome—you just have to know how to use it to your advantage. When looking for your next opportunity, job, or career after a failed startup experience, don't look back on it as lost time. Others around you don't have that experience in their back pocket. They probably don't know what it's like to go from zero to one. In life, you either win or you learn—there's no losing. And when you learn from your experiences, you're guaranteed to have a much better experience the second time around. You develop scar tissue, own your mistakes, and adapt to unforeseen circumstances, all the while building confidence. Your experience will go a long way when you decide to build another startup from the ground up.

2. Do not underestimate the power of being a student or a recent graduate. Knowing this, you can bear a lot of risks even if your startup doesn't work out and you have to find a new position—there will always be people out there who can help you or vouch for you. The student card can go a long, long way. Whether it's finding grants or finding fellowships for a career interest of yours, there's an endless number of resources at your fingertips. Also, cold emails, tweets, and outreach all work a lot better when you're young and hungry. People are more willing to help you when you're a student or recent graduate, mainly because it shows you're still learning. If you're not a student, show that you're willing to learn and that you're a hustler. It'll go a long way.

3. You don't have the inherent risks that many people do when working on a startup—as a student, you shouldn't have to worry too much about failure. A big reason people don't start companies is because of the risk. Time, money, kids, career. There's a lot out there; it's what makes building in college so attractive. What's the risk? Your parents (or your student loans) are covering your finances for four years, and you can learn and do whatever you want for four years. You have a safety net and can try whatever you'd like. That's a lot of time, and you don't have to worry about your potential failure affecting those around you (your future kids, spouse, etc.). Take the risk while you can and don't think about your startup potentially failing.

#1 Lesson Learned: Plan for the worst and expect the best: always hedge your bets and make sure you both mentally and professionally prepare yourself for what could happen.

About the Author: The author is a recent graduate from UT Austin with a BS in mechanical engineering. During their time at UT Austin, they co-founded a city-to-city transportation company that aimed to increase EV adoption and make travel more efficient.

FROM ENTREPRENEURSHIP TO CAREER BY CHELSEA AND JUSTIN

Regardless of what happens with your company, I guarantee your startup experience will help your career. This is true for a few reasons:

1. It's hands-on learning. No matter what aspect of the startup you support, you're getting real-world experience you can put on your resume.

2. It's adding years to your professional experience.

3. It's amazing for communication and team-building skills (which all employers love right now).

4. It grows your network—you'll meet tons of new people who could introduce you to your next gig.

My startup led me here, to writing this book, which is totally wild to think about. I had no idea what the decision to start a company in college would lead to. It's not something you necessarily plan for, but it surprises you in the very best ways. During my time with my startup, I met the person who would give me my next job. Then, I was connected to the local startup community where I initially volunteered, then found a full-time position helping other entre-preneurs. With that experience, I was able to join Techstars and help startup founders on a global scale. Hindsight is twenty-twenty, so today, my story makes sense. It's almost like I planned it! But I definitely did not. The only rules I followed were:

1. Work with good people you enjoy being around.

2. Work on something you care about.

3. Find a way to help others/give back.

4. Take opportunities (maybe not all of them, but the good ones).

5. Have fun!

Starting a company in college is a gateway to a fulfilling career, whether you stay with your company or move on to something else. The stories in this final chapter further illustrate the bright future an entrepreneurial experience can lead to.

FEATURED STORY:
Chelsea LaFerla,
Founder, Petitas, USC, MSc
in Entrepreneurship
and Innovation,
Graduated 2018

I remember walking into my first business school mixer at USC. I was faced with a room full of men dressed in neatly pressed and perfectly tailored suits while my outfit was a dress from the Nordstrom teen department. My confidence was a bit shaken, and I began to feel out of place. I knew I never wanted to feel that way again, and soon after, I embarked on a journey to empower petite women through fashion. My goal was for every woman five-foot-five and under to be "clothed in confidence" through uniquely tailored, high-end garments that could take women from desk to dinner. The clothes were ethically and sustainably made in the United States using premium, hand-made fabrics.

I came from a long line of Italian tailors and seamstresses, and grew up sewing clothes with my grandmother, a skilled seamstress and wedding dress designer. While I grew up around textiles, I did not know just how much work went into designing and launching a fashion brand, especially one with unique sizing. Finding a pattern-maker and US-based manufacturing team was no small feat. I remember knocking on fifty doors before finding the production team who would help me create our first batch of clothes. After numerous rounds of edits (and lots of trial and error), we produced our first line. I was so excited, and the community around me was incredibly supportive. At our early boutiques, however, I'd hear women praising the garments' fit and style, but not the price. Back to the drawing board. How could I ensure our workers were paid fair wages and make high-end garments while still making enough of a profit to grow the business? This and many other questions kept me up at night as each batch of clothing brought along a new struggle. I'd work through issues ranging from fit and turnaround time, to pricing and inventory.

After numerous rounds (and helpful guidance from mentors at USC and Blackstone's LaunchPad Lift), I launched a line that had the magic three: fit, price, and style. Pieces sold quickly and our growing petite community gave glowing reviews. While our line was gaining success and recognition from both consumers and retail buyers, I had to make perhaps the hardest decision of my life: I moved on. My greatest joy doing Petitas was knowing that we'd been able to clothe women, just like me, with confidence while also paying our production team fair wages. But as I spoke with retail industry experts and began looking at the long-term financial trajectory of Petitas, I knew it was time to close shop.

What was next? Through the USC and Techstars network, I landed a position working for an up-and-coming financial technology startup that I was incredibly excited about. During my two years with the startup, I served as director of marketing and eventually sales, gaining cross-functional experience that would prepare me for my current role as founding member and sales head at Tatem, a business to business, software as a service company that focuses on helping other startup founders (like me at Petitas) solve some of their most tedious and difficult problems.

What I didn't realize was just how much Petitas had prepared me for these later opportunities. By serving in almost every role, from operations and sales to marketing and product development, I was able to fast-forward my business knowledge. I gained experience that might have taken more than four years in a traditional job in less than half the time. As a founder and team manager, I also quickly learned how skills like good communication, leadership, and careful planning come into play. These and other skills served as a foundation for accelerating my career growth and understanding future positions.

TOP THREE TAKEAWAYS:

My three tips for anyone looking to transfer experience gained as a startup founder to their next position are as follows:

1. Always maintain a founder mindset. By that, I mean take ownership of your role. That requires being a self-starter, figuring things out on your own, and taking the initiative to personally ensure the results you or your company want.

2. Lead with humble confidence. During my time at Petitas, I realized just how important confidence is. A lack of confidence/feeling unsure affects the whole team. I've found that it's always better to jump out and take risks and apologize later (if needed). But the humility aspect is key. Be ready (and open) to be wrong and accept mistakes you've made as part of the learning process.

3. Treat your clients and colleagues as if they were your own (family or friends). When I moved into sales, I decided to treat every client as if the company was my own like at Petitas. That meant giving them the time, respect, and nurturing they needed, and not clocking out at 6 p.m. Because of that, I built close relationships with our clientele, which reflected positively on our company. That mindset also helped me gain grounded, positive relationships with my colleagues because I treated them as if I were at the helm: taking the initiative to invest in our relationships, see how they were doing, and ask how I might help them along.

#1 Lesson Learned: If you're thinking of doing a startup, do it. It's worth all the time and sacrifice. You'll end up learning far more with a startup than at an established company.

About Chelsea: Chelsea built an e-commerce fashion brand from the ground up and grew it to $12,000 in sales in year one as a part of Blackstone's LaunchPad Lift program before becoming the director of marketing and eventually sales at a financial technology startup.

If there's one thing I learned from my experience with my (failed) startup, it's that careers are more like jungle gyms than ladders (perhaps stolen from Sheryl Sandberg). Even though my startup didn't become my full-time job, it led me to a fulfilling career where I love what I do every day. I leveraged my startup experience to help other founders (just like you) and use it as a tool to embark on a whole new career. I wanted to share some deeper insights into leveraging your startup experience to advance your career, and I couldn't imagine a better contributor to write about this than my colleague Justin. Justin had a dynamic career as a product manager-turned-founder. In the pages that follow, Justin talks about how you can think of your career as a prototype, just like a product. It's something that can be tested, adjusted, and redirected. I hope you find inspiration for your career in Justin's words, and discover ways to build an amazing future for yourself, whether it's with a startup or something else.

EVERYTHING IS A PROTOTYPE: INCLUDING YOUR CAREER
by **Justin Lokitz,**
Advisor, Author, and Cofounder of Formation Creative and Plantfully

Whether I'm teaching MBA students, advising startup founders, or working with employees and interns in one of my own companies, the question I'm asked most is, "How might I go about changing (or pivoting) my career?" While thousands of books have been written on this subject, my answer is simple: Prototype what that role might look and feel like before you ever actually make the change.

Like working a summer internship at a tech company, prototyping a new career is really no more than finding something you're interested in, finding someone who does that already, and then finding a way to help them do what they do (for free most of the time). It can be done super-cheaply and even while still in school or working at another job.

This process is basically deliberately designing your career. To understand what that means, it's best to first start with the definition of design.

Design is an iterative process that starts with understanding the world around you; from that understanding, you might create some ideas; those ideas are tested (validated or invalidated) via prototypes; then, with enough information—and having validated or invalidated your idea—you either pivot or decide to continue moving forward. Essentially, design is the scientific method for business...and other things that aren't exactly science.

When you look at every challenge or potential life-changing question as a design problem, it becomes easier to create a course of action that will help you determine what's right for you. And, when it comes to design, once you've formulated what you believe you want to do next, whether that's founding a startup or starting a new career as X, your next step is to prototype what that might look like.

When it comes to design, the goal should not be to prescribe a form or function arbitrarily. We want our choices to be informed by the way people actually use our products/services, so we start with an initial hypothesis, then use prototypes, or preliminary mockups, early on in the process to collect hands-on data to better craft the experience moving forward. The idea is to test and learn often. Mind you, prototypes—sometimes also called pretotypes—shouldn't be engineering quality. They're just meant to test an idea or assumption.

Similarly, when it comes to your next career, you can and should find ways to test what that career might look like before you jump into the deep end. By prototyping first, you might even test multiple careers simultaneously before you ever make a decision about which path to take.

For example, before I co-founded BMI Americas, the US office of a global business design and strategy firm, headquartered in Amsterdam, I worked at Autodesk as a senior product manager, overseeing most of the geospatial and planning software products. Although I knew I wanted to do something on my own, rather than quitting my paying job (or starting something in stealth), I booked some vacation days to help run a few business model innovation workshops with Patrick van der Pijl, the CEO of BMI International, whom I met through the MBA in Design Strategy program when he was a guest speaker in my Innovation Studio course.

I treated this work as a personal prototype, meaning I started with assumptions about the work I'd be doing, and even sent those assumptions to my manager at Autodesk so he knew what I (thought I) would be doing. This was also my way of keeping every-thing above board. When I got to the workshop, I didn't just hang back and watch. I worked with Patrick to understand the flow and where I could insert myself. Because Patrick was the expert and could manage the entire workshop without me, I was confident that even if I failed at parts, I wouldn't ruin the entire workshop. After every design sprint (about one and half hours), I would check in with Patrick to see how I did and to decide (together) whether I should dive even deeper in the following design sprint.

After workshops, I would do a bigger postmortem with Patrick, where I would solicit super-candid feedback. All of this prototyping really just helped me understand what would be in store for me should I take that path and what I would need to get better at. Was this what I wanted to be doing? Was I any good at it? Was it worth pursuing?

And...I've never stopped prototyping. Today, I find I'm constantly prototyping what tomorrow might look like. From new ventures I'm interested in launching to the ventures I've been working in/ on for a while, I consider everything I do a prototype. Which is to say, when I look at everything as something that can be improved upon, I'm never afraid to fail. In fact, I often learn way more by failing (or invalidating) something than I would if I succeeded at that thing. And so can you!

Now that you've read this awesome book (which I wish I would have had when I was in university), consider not just how you're going to launch your startup while still a student, but rather how you might prototype what that will look like for you. What are the small steps you can take that will provide you with a window to your future self? Whom might you connect with who is already doing something similar? How might you gain quick and honest feedback from your own personal prototype?

In my opinion, the best thing you can do when considering what to do next is to follow the design process and prototype your prospective futures before diving in. Then you'll learn by actually doing the job (or at least parts of it), rather than just researching it. After all, not all dream jobs turn out to be good dreams.

My big question to you is: What career are you going to proto-type tomorrow?

About Justin: Justin is the author of the best-selling books, *Design A Better Business: New Tools, Skills and Mindset for Strategy and Innovation and Business Model Shifts: Six Ways to Create New Value for Customers*, a startup entrepreneur and advisor, an MBA professor, a technologist, the cofounder and CTO/COO of Formation Creative, and the founder and CEO of Plantfully. He has more than two decades of experience designing and executing strategies for large, multinational corporations, and several startups, including his own.

Justin has an MBA in design strategy, from California College of the Arts, a BA in environmental science and geography, from the University of California Santa Barbara, and professional certifications in software development and product management from the University of California Berkeley.

A FINAL NOTE

I hope you've enjoyed reading the stories in this book.

I hope you feel inspired and motivated to go start something great.

I hope you understand the ways your university can help you along the way.

I hope you see how entrepreneurship can lead to an exciting and fulfilling career, regardless of what happens to your company.

These stories are just the start. The student-founder experience is evolving, and I don't plan to stop sharing stories now! If you have a story you'd like to share, contact me at www.students-start.com.

Go confidently!

Courtney

ABOUT THE AUTHOR
Courtney Gras

Courtney has developed and managed programs that help entrepreneurs succeed for nearly a decade. She started this work after spending eight years with the startup company she founded in college. Courtney has worked locally in the Northeast Ohio startup community where she is based, at Techstars as director for the LaunchPad student entrepreneurship network and director on the Ecosystem team, and at Amazon Web Services as Startup Community Lead. Courtney is passionate about helping student founders everywhere and compiled this book so every student can have the confidence to start something amazing.

Courtney began her startup journey when she was an undergraduate engineering student. Courtney worked on her cleantech startup for eight years—while studying full time, while working at co-op jobs, and after she graduated when she got a dream job at NASA. She was named to the Forbes 30 Under 30 for her work in cleantech. **But her startup failed.**

Through failure, Courtney found a passion for helping young founders avoid the pitfalls she faced when starting her company. Courtney has built global programs that impact hundreds of thousands of early-stage entrepreneurs, facilitated thousands of mentor connections, and invented new ways to connect founders in a virtual world. Courtney believes in putting founders first and giving first. She continues to mentor founders, volunteer in her local startup community, and speak on the topic of student entrepreneurship at universities around the world.

To get in touch with Courtney, visit www.courtneygras.com, or follow her on Twitter: @courtneyagras

THE ULTIMATE RESOURCE LIST AND COMMUNITY

RESOURCE LIST:

I know that finding good resources as a student-founder can be a daunting experience. With nearly infinite options, where do you even start? To help take away some of the guesswork, we've compiled a list of go-to resources from student-founders and other contributors who built this book.

COMMUNITY:

I also know that being a student-founder can be a lonely journey. That's why we launched an online community to accompany this book. The community offers a safe space to ask questions, get the help you need, find even more resources, and connect with like-minded student founders across the globe.

To access the resource list and join our community, visit
www.students-start.com

Made in the USA
Middletown, DE
24 March 2022